A Jamaica Poor No More

by Michael Irving Phillips

Published by Hot Calaloo Press, December 2019
Copyright © 2019 Michael Irving Phillips
ISBN 0-9610516-3-9

Dedication

This book is dedicated to the overseas Jamaicans, who despite living abroad, continue to maintain a keen interest in Jamaica and involve themselves in helping out in so many ways. Some of these Jamaicans run the myriad of Jamaican organisations which keep the Jamaican culture and concerns alive. Others organize doctors and other medical personnel to come to Jamaica to donate their services to operate badly needed free medical clinics in various regions of Jamaica, often year after year.

Table of Contents

Introduction

Jamaica has problems. This book does not babble about them but comes up with unique solutions to these problems. From over twenty five years of writing the Hot Calaloo newsletter about Jamaica and the rest of the Caribbean, I have maintained and acute knowledge and perspective which I have brought to this book.

How come developing countries never develop? Jamaica is in that pack. Will Jamaica develop in five years, ten years, ever? I think there is acceptance of Jamaica poor forever. Not only that, but there is hope that she will never go bankrupt like Puerto Rico has. In 1954 Jamaica was the leading exporter of bauxite in the world. Now, in 2019, her rating is very low. Once the US dollar was less than the Jamaican dollar. Now the Jamaican dollar is less than one US cent!

The fact is, if Jamaica and other developing countries do like they have been doing, they will be forever poor. But by following the revolutionary economic policy as detailed in my book, *A Jamaica Poor No More*, Jamaica will become poor no more. Jamaica has been begging for scraps from our economic masters. But, no more. With our new economic policy of Jamaicanism, Jamaica will be standing proud, poor no more, begging for scraps no more.

The book introduces Jamaicanism and applies the Goodwill Revolution to make Jamaica have, not just a high quality of life, but among the highest in the world.

Jamaicanism will fix the poverty problem, but that is not the only problem.

All over the world a rat race culture pits people against one another in a competition to get as much money, materials, and power as they can. This rat race culture is driven by the love of money. This is not good. After all, the love of money is the root of all evil. Greed, selfishness, ruthlessness and avarice are assets in the money-hogging rat race culture. Kindness, sincerity, compassion are liabilities. The rat race culture has corrupted our values and our institutions. The winners of the rat race are highly respected. Losers are despised. If there are ten participants in any race, there is only one winner, but nine losers. Similarly, the rat race creates lots of losers. This is unacceptable.

Unfortunately, most people think the rat race is compulsory. But, we do have a choice. Simply dropping out is not really a solution. Jamaica needs to choose a real alternative to the rat race. The Goodwill Revolution is that alternative. The rat race culture is deeply entrenched so it will take a revolution, a cultural revolution, hence the Goodwill-to-all revolution.

The Goodwill Revolution encompasses a comprehensive set of principles which reinforces and mobilizes the inherent goodness of mankind as the key to true happiness. In the Goodwill Revolution, kindness, compassion, and honesty are valuable assets. Greed, selfishness, ruthlessness are liabilities.

So the book advocates Jamaicanism to fix the economic problems and also the rejection of the money-hogging rat race to adopt the Goodwill Revolution in order to fix the cultural problems.

Chapter 1

Non-developing Countries

Insanity

Jamaica is not a poor country. We do not have poor countries anymore. Instead we have developing countries. Nice euphemism. So, Jamaica is a developing country. The sad fact is developing countries are not developing and Jamaica is no exception. The greatest problem these countries face is poverty. Do they have a plan to eradicate poverty in five, ten, twenty years or ever? The most likely answer is ever, which in reality means never. It has been a near impossible task despite best of intentions.

But Jamaica can do it if they follow my proposal. We have been locked into policies that have not worked and will never work. We have followed the advice of the vaunted International Monetary Fund (IMF) and other international experts. Right now as I write Chile and Haiti are burning because they are trying to carry out IMF requirement to obtain IMF loans. Let me show you in this book how to get real help from the IMF instead of extortion.

Once these international experts told us that a country had to possess iron and coal industry to be prosperous. Not anymore.

Then these international experts told us that a country had to possess a strong manufacturing base to be prosperous. America shifted its manufacturing base to China and some other cheap labor countries. But China is becoming prosperous. Obviously these international experts are not infallible.

Then these international experts told Jamaica and other developing countries that the way to prosperity was foreign investments. Jamaica needed to increase its manufacturing base. Traditionally, to increase manufacturing, Jamaica tries to entice foreign corporations to set up there by offering tax breaks and other benefits. She has to compete with other developing countries so they make the benefits very attractive but often at considerable expense to the country. Now, if the foreign corporation analyses the prospects and foresees enormous profits, then it will set up in Jamaica. Jamaica will benefit with some employment and a relatively small financial gains. These gains compared to the huge profits of the foreign corporation are mere crumbs. Has this plan worked?

Well the prime model for this plan in the Caribbean was Puerto Rico. Furthermore as a commonwealth of the United States, this was an additional advantage there. Did this plan work in Puerto Rico? Today Puerto Rico is bankrupt even before they were devastated by hurricane Maria. Government pensions are in trouble. They had to layoff many government employees . They had to close over one hundred and seventy- nine schools in 2017 because of budget problems. That year, Puerto Rico had $73 billion in public debt. By comparison, the U.S. city of Detroit had less than $20 billion in debt when it filed for bankruptcy in 2013, which was the biggest U.S. municipal bankruptcy ever.

So Puerto Rico had to surrender most of its already restricted autonomy to the US in order to settle its debts. They were forced to agree to The Puerto Rico Oversight, Management, and Economic Stability Act (PROMESA), a process for restructuring debt, and expedited procedures for approving critical infrastructure projects. Through PROMESA, the US Congress established an unelected Fiscal Control Board (FCB) to oversee the debt restructuring. The FCB's approved fiscal austerity plan for 2017-2026, cut deeply into the Puerto Rican public service budget—included cuts to health care, pensions, and education—in order to repay creditors.

Although Puerto Rico was bankrupt, it was not allowed to declare bankruptcy. In bankruptcy creditors often get a percentage of their money owed instead of full payment. But not for PROMESA, as creditor corporations continued to get their full monthly payments while workers bore the brunt. For example, one of the most controversial provisions of PROMESA was the reduction of the federal minimum wage from $7.25 to $4.25 an hour for workers 25 years old and younger. The last time hourly wages were this low was about 20 years ago.

Obviously this traditional plan did not work for Puerto Rico. If it did not work here, the prospects of it ever working in Jamaica or anywhere else are dim. But, still we persist. The definition of insanity is doing the same thing over and over and expecting different results. How long shall we pursue this folly? *How long, Oh Lord, how long?*

Chapter 2

Jamaica's Downward Economic Spiral

Following that Jamaica-poor-forever plan, and despite well -meaning politicians, conditions in Jamaica have gotten worse over the years. Politicians have gotten a lot of the blame, but it is that economic system that is responsible. In that system Jamaica's main source of income, on which she depends so much, exports, have been going downhill.

Sugar

I remember in Jamaica, many years ago when it seemed there were large cane fields everywhere. I remember the burning of canefields to make cane-cutting easier. I remember slow-moving carts laden with cane, impeding the traffic as they transported the cane to sugar factories. Not anymore.

The Sugar Industry is the oldest continually operating industry in Jamaica and has been the largest employer of labour. But new international globalism rules have been very unkind to sugar in Jamaica and the rest of the Caribbean. Both prices on the world market and production have fallen precipitously as depicted in the chart below:

Year	1975	1980	11990	2000	2010	2017
Tons	366,411	250,676	219,070	216,387	121,806	87,993

Bananas
(This article I wrote for Hot Calaloo, 2007)
Banana Wars, Banana Memories
What is the most popular fruit eaten here in America? Yes, it is the banana. Traditionally, throughout the West Indies,

it has been an agriculture crop second only to sugar. However, banana wars with Latin America loom a threat to a tradition, a way of life.

I remember that first morning many years ago. I was just a boy of about ten spending my summer holidays in the countryside, the little Jamaican north coast port town of Oracabessa. On that memorable morning, I looked out the window of my uncle's house which offered a spectacular panoramic view of the harbor. There "It" was, almost filling the entire harbor and horizon. "It" was the "banana boat". To my young and tender eyes, it seemed massive, magnificent. It could have well been the luxury liner the Queen Mary, instead of the Jamaica Producer. It had come in overnight.

The sleepy little port had been transformed into a hum of activity. I was excited. It seemed to me that everyone in the town was somehow involved. The mood was festive. The smell of money, no doubt. Trucks overladen with bunches of banana, wrapped in banana leaves, steadily streamed into port. Since Oracabessa was not a deep water harbor , the 'Banana boat" could not come up to the dock, but had to drop anchor outside. So the "six-hand seven-hand bunches' had to be loaded assembly-line style by vigorous perspiring men unto small boats which transported them out to the 'banana boat'! As the men worked they sang. Of course, it was not reggae, which was decades away in the future. It was not even calypso, but traditional Jamaican work songs. songs like Day-o, Hill and Gully, and Sammy Dead. This continued non-stop way into the night. I remember looking out from the veranda on that starlit night with fascination as the flickering lights of the flotilla of tiny banana-laden boats made   their   way   to   the   huge   ship. That summer I really came to know the banana. From the short stubby "Cbiney" banana to the slender but durable Lackatan to the robust Robusta and Gros Mitchell. Do you remember rips banana fritters, fnied and boiled green bananas? How about mackerel and banana rundown also known as 'Dip-n Fall Back'!? I even had "banana water" to which was attributed all sorts of nutritional powers. But, I hated banana porridge.

Survivors

Banana like the people of Jamaica and the rest of the West Indies are survivors. Threatened regularly and sometimes devastated by hurricane, but they survive. Threatened by disease, but with extensive help from our agricultural researchers, they adapt and survive. In the past, in order for the West Indies to survive, the banana had to survive. But will the banana trade in the West Indies survive? Sadly, USA prospects don't seem good. The fight is being waged primarily by the Windward Isles, who are especially dependent on this for employment and foreign exchange. They are up against powerful multinational corporations with banana plantations in Latin America.

The bottom line is that these Latin American countries are able to grow it cheaper and these Caribbean countries must depend on the protected market of the UK. But, the UK is not as independent as it used to be now that it is a member of the European Common Market (EC). So far, Britain has been barely able to beat back the attacks of other EC countries led by Germany, Belgium and the Netherlands as well as the Latin American and African producers against this protected market. I, myself, am surprised at the fight Britain has put up on behalf of the Caribbean countries even though it means more expensive bananas for the English consumer. Upcoming General Agreement on Trade and Tariffs (GATT), and LOME talks are expected to take dead aim on this protected market again.

Effects

Up till now, the West Indies has been moving closer to its Latin American neighbors. But, these banana wars are straining relations in some circles. The Windward Islands governments of Grenada, St. Lucia, St Vincent and the Grenadines, and Dominica, have even threatened to pull out of the Organisation of American States (OAS) over this issue. Banana prices in Grenada have dropped to their lowest since 1985. There is no question a way of life for many is being threatened. Not one single banana we eat here in the US comes from the West Indies. The market belongs exclusively to the Latin American countries. The UK is virtually the only export market for West Indian bananas. Now that is imperiled.

I went back to Oracabessa. The "banana boat" has long abandoned it, lured away by a deep sea port elsewhere. Instead, on the distant horizon, occasionally a tourist laden luxury ocean liner can be barely discerned heading probability for nearby Ocho Rios. And, from time to time, small boats can be seen dropping or retrieving their fish pots, but their message is *"Oh yes we have no bananas, we've got no bananas today. "* Tourism has had some impact, but the town remains a sleepy fishing village. Unemployment seems high. Of course, traditional work songs no longer fill the air. That day, I could not help but notice a man clad in a flamboyant gold and black sequined dance-hall costume. In the background I could hear a sound system blaring with its deep thumping bass " ... *gal yuh body good, it good Iike a gold. ..... "*

Sadly, the banana republic days are no more. Like sugar, it also lost its protected status internationally. Its export market fell on hard times. Here are some lamentable statisticsabout banana production according to Actualitix World Atlas:

Years	1966	1980	1990	2000	2013
Tons	240,000	140,000	127,660	102,000	37,211

Bauxite

Bauxite has been an important source of income for Jamaica. By 1957 Jamaica was the leading bauxite producer in the world. with a production capacity of nearly 5 million tons of bauxite per year, almost a quarter of all the bauxite mined in the world in that year. In 1961 there were four companies mining bauxite in Jamaica In 1974 Jamaica bauxite was the second largest producer of bauxite and the second largest exporter of alumina in the world behind Australia. Those were the good old days.

 Over the next ten years, the island that was once the number one exporter of bauxite had fallen to about sixth place and producing 14.6 million tons of bauxite, about a mere 7% of the world bauxite production. Things have gotten even worse. By 2017, with a levy of US$1.50 per metric ton plus a US$0.50 per metric ton royalty, bauxite brings in only about US$3.8 million. And, this pittance is probably one of the top sources of income for Jamaica, for which Jamaica is so grateful.

The Jamaican Dollar

Do you remember pounds, shillings and pence? Well the Jamaica dollar replaced that old English currency. At that time the Jamaica dollar was worth more than the American dollar. Seventy seven cents in Jamaican currency was equal to one US dollar. But over the years, the Jamaican dollar has tumbled so low that a Jamaican dollar is worth less than a single US cent and it is still falling.

In 1972 one US dollar was equal to 77 Jamaica cents. Yes the Jamaican dollar was actually worth more than the yankee dollar. How things have changed! By the year 1992 one US doller was equal to Ja$22.22, by 2012 Ja$100 and by 2018 US$1 is equal to Ja$125 and still falling. The once proud Jamaican dollar is now worth less than a US cent. Jamaica is not alone by any means but this precipitous decline is a nightmare.

Year	1972	1992	2012	2018
1 US dollar	Ja$ 0.77	Ja$22.22	Ja$100	Ja$125

Third World Debt

Many developing countries, desperate to come up with enough money to pay their civil servants, teachers, police, nurses, doctors, come on their knees to agencies like the the International Monetary Fund (IMF), World Bank and World Trade Organization (WTO)..Many of these countries and billions of people are devastated under the burden of debt and trade policies to which they must submit. The developing world now spends $1.3 on debt repayment for every $1 it receives in grants. For example, Nigeria borrowed around $5 billion and has paid about $16 billion, but still owes $28 billion. In 1999, $128 million was transferred from the poorest countries to the richest for debt repayments What a racket!

Unfortunately, Jamaica is stuck in this racket. The IMF lends Jamaica US$2 billion. To round off the figures, let's say that is equal to J$200 billion. Then the Jamaican dollar declines as it has been doing. The loan becomes a noose around Jamaica's neck for as the Jamaican dollar depreciates, this means the money owed increases instead of getting lower despite payments. Besides, the IMF money comes with strings. They make conditions which affect public financial spending. Some of these conditions can be very draconian such as firing civil servants, cutting salaries of nurses and so on. It is a remarkable feat that Jamaica has been able to survive these loans.

Jamaica for Jamaicans only

One of the dire consequences of this precipitous decline of the Jamaican currency is the effect on real estate sales. As the currency rate drops, Jamaican real estate becomes more expensive to Jamaicans and cheaper to foreigners with stable currency. At this rate, foreigners can gobble up Jamaican real estate for peanuts, and rent it back to Jamaicans. The more those currency rich foreigners buy up Jamaican real estate, the more expensive it would become and thus the less Jamaicans could afford it with their weak currency. Big prosperous strong-currency countries like America and EU countries would never face such a risk. So, currency devaluation could dispossess Jamaicans of their own land. I see no way out of this potential dilemma other than making the buying and selling of real estate limited to Jamaican citizens only. This seems drastic, but I see no alternative.

.

Chapter 3

Jamaicanism - A Pathway to Prosperity

It is painfully obvious that under the present economic system Jamaica will be poor forever. A Jamaica poor forever or A Jamaica poor no more. The choice is perpetual poverty or an end to poverty. The solution is not capitalism. It is not communism. It is not socialism. It is a completely new –ism which is unique to Jamaica, so I call it Jamaicanism. Under Jamaicanism, my proposed economic system, Jamaica will be poor no more.

Foreign and local corporations make money in Jamaica. These corporations get rich in Jamaica. So, Jamaica government must form its own corporation too in order to get rich also. This Jamaica Government. Corporation(JGC) will compete with the other corporations so it will be no puny company. By necessity it will start out small but its goal is to be the largest and most efficient corporation in Jamaica with subsidiaries all over the island. It will not follow civil service rules but will follow the rules and practices of corporations. Existing corporations do not really care about Jamaica, but only for making a profit for their shareholders. The Jamaica Government Corporation will care about making a profit, but their primary goal is caring about the citizens of Jamaica.

One of the first reactions to this idea was that "the Jamaica government could not even run a patty shop". This was not completely unexpected. This is a popular stereotype of government.

 I myself have encountered such a problem. Once on my return to the US from a vacation in Jamaica, I found myself stuck with a lot of Jamaican money. I am sure this happens to a lot of tourists. So I thought, " why not set up a charity collection box in the airport so that departing tourists could donate their Jamaican money before they flew back to their home"? I suggested this by mail to government officials. I even sought the assistance of persons of influence there in Jamaica that I knew personally. Finally I got a positive response. I was elated and could not wait to see this put into effect the next time I went back to Jamaica. I had to search the airport diligently but finally I found it. It was a very inconspicuous brown box with a slot to insert money. "Is this it? I thought. I had no Jamaican money so I decided to donate a few American dollars. I could not get the money through the slot!

Years later, I was in Dublin airport, Ireland. There was my donation box. It was no puny inconspicuous box. It was a prominently-displayed transparent artistic plastic globe that I am sure attracted tourists to donate their left-over euros.

I have also encountered charges of cronyism and corruption would undermine this government corporations. To be sure, these are also real problems. But, they are not insurmountable. They exist in the present keep-Jamaica-poor system and should not stifle or prevent us from adopting a system to take Jamaica on the road to prosperity. Besides, awareness of these problems and setting up government as a corporation will minimize these problems.

The old school, stuck- in-their-ways, will not run this government corporation. Instead the corporation will seek out new innovative committed leaders who will recognize that the destiny of Jamaica is in their hands. Consequently, one of the most important officers will be a Director of Innovation, who will be charged with considering the feasibility of latest computer technology for application to the variety of industries.

I remember a long time ago when the British had and ran the Suez Canal. When the Egyptians took it over, there was a feeling that they could not administer it. But they did, and even better than the British. There is an element of that here now, a feeling that Jamaicans cannot do it as well as the foreign corporations. We shall not be undermined by such imposed inferiority complex. "A prophet is without honour in his own country." We are not just seeking parity. Instead, our motto will be, "Anything they can do, we can do better". Or, at least we shall always try to do it better.

 Jamaicans have excelled internationally in many fields. For example, Jamaican Ann-Marie Campbell, executive vice president of United States Home Depot stores, has been ranked as the 16th most powerful woman in the world for 2018 by Fortune Magazine. In her role as executive vice president, she has responsibility for some 2,000 Home Depot stores throughout the US. Campbell cites her Jamaican heritage as a major reason for her success.

Even our much maligned civil service workers do not get the credit they deserve at home. But, they are recognized internationally. Our public sector workers have been hailed for their contribution to the country's positive performance in the 2017-2018 Global Competitiveness Report, which shows that Jamaica is ranked 27 out of 140 countries in labour market efficiency.

This Jamaica Government Corporation will enter into any enterprise in which it analyses and foresees a healthy profit. Big corporations have diversified into a variety of fields to become conglomerates. Do you remember when General Electric was a company which made refrigerators, stoves and other appliances? Well now General Electric Company (GE) is an American multinational conglomerate incorporated in New York. As of 2018, it operates through the following segments: aviation, healthcare, power, renewable energy, digital industry, additive manufacturing, venture capital and finance, lighting, transportation, and oil and gas.

Likewise, JGC will be a conglomerate with companies all over the island involved in tourism, agriculture, housing and all sorts of businesses. They will have sole proprietorships, partnerships with other companies or even individuals. Like corporations they will even buy out other companies. Let me emphasize that all transactions with other companies or individuals will be voluntary and without compulsion. In time, JGC will have a wide network of companies and businesses all over the island for the benefit of Jamaica and the Jamaican people.

JGC shall include sole proprietorships, partnerships, franchises, franchisors, active investments and passive investments. Partnerships are very important as there would be many partnerships all over the island. The attraction of partnerships between companies and individuals and JGC will provide the expertise and means to increase profits and JGC will then receive a percentage of the increased profits, It is a win-win situation for both parties. If profits do not increase, then the partner would pay nothing to JGC, but would only pay if profits increase. In other partnerships JGC will benefit from the expertise of the partner, always for the mutual satisfaction of both. Foreign corporations that funnel money out of Jamaica, like Uber, fast food chains and even real estate companies. would be primary targets of JGC competition.

This book provides only the framework and direction of these business arrangements. The exact details are beyond the scope as they would depend on the specific circumstances of each agreement.

Agriculture Business

Jamaica is an agricultural country. An agricultural country is almost synonymous with poverty. Farmers in Jamaica basically eke out a living. Even in prosperous America, the family farm is a dying business. Despite state-of-the art agriculture machinery and high tech methods, according to The Hightower Lowdown, May 2019,the 2018 median farm income for US farm households was a minus $1,553 (Net Farm Income is the money left over after a farm family subtracts the cost of producing their crops from the amount they get paid for them.) They can't even break even. Why?

It is because corporate middlemen, commodity speculators and monopolistic wholesalers dominate the market and control the prices paid to the farmers.

Everywhere n the US, the family farm is being replaced by agribusiness. But, here in Jamaica in my proposal, the farmers will team up with JGC to form agribusiness for the benefit of all. No longer will the government just advise farmers but it will serve as a business partner in a profit making venture in a unique relationship which I call Partnership With People (PWP).

So JGC will team up with farmers to create agribusiness in which the agricultural industry will engage in the producing operations of a farm, the manufacture and distribution of farm equipment and supplies, and the processing, storage, and distribution of farm commodities.

Objectives

- Provide food needs of Jamaica
- Make a profit
- Fair price to farmers
- Reduce the importation of food
- Increase yields through technology and research

Focus Areas

- Seek value-added food processing. For example with the fore mentioned yellow yam, JGC would investigate the feasibility of yam chips, like potato and banana chips. In America I have found potato bread in supermarkets. Could there be yam bread from yam flower? Recently cassava is used in the production of Red Stripe beer.
- Marketing
    - Foreign
    - Local – supermarkets, hotels, restaurants

- Collection and storage
- Agri-technology – greenhouse. Irrigation. pest control, fertilizer, etc.
- Provide a guaranteed price to farmers
- Mechanisation

Jamaica Hotel Business

Tourism is a vital industry in Jamaica. So, the Jamaica Business Corporation should be deeply involved in the hotel business. This business is complex and very competitive. But, it is not rocket science. So, with the proper commitment, expertise and training, Jamaica can compete with Hilton, Hyatt, Sheraton or any of the big hotel guns. Why should foreign hotel corporations essentially get the lion's share of our tourism market? We need a new attitude. Unfortunately, the fact is we have been wasting opportunities.

Hotels have crashed and burned over the years with the government trying to rescue them. For instance, in 2009 the Breeze Montego Bay Hotel bit the dust and closed. Jamaica rescued it by buying it and up to 2019 it remained shuttered. In 2011 it went up for sale with a valuation of US$14.32 million. Now in 2018 it is reported to be in the process of being sold for US$7.8 million. In about a decade, this property did not appreciate, but instead lost about US$6 million dollars. This is Jamaica-poor-forever policy. I am sure the new buyer will make a mint. If the new buyer can make a mint, then JGC can make a mint too. Why wait until the property value falls by over US$6 million?

Auto Dealership Business

This is a perfect business for the JGC. They would have an automatic large customer base – the government vehicles, busses, cars, vans, trucks etcetera. They would acquire and repair these vehicles. Of course they would not be limited to government vehicles only, but would also provide quality service to the general public at competitive rates.

Housing Construction and Rental Business

A popular route individuals have amassed fortunes is by real estate .business. This include not just the buying and selling of commercial and residential property but also the renting of property. The Jamaica corporation should become the landlord of Jamaica. Not only will the corporation achieve great wealth but Jamaicans will receive a fairer deal. So far, the Government providing of houses has been essentially limited to low income housing to enable poor people to obtain a home. Why should the government be restricted to the unprofitable provision of homes for the poor? It is time to provide housing for all socioeconomic groups and at a profit. Let the profits come rolling in for the benefit of all Jamaica.

Secondhand Clothing Business

As department store after department store goes bankrupt in America because of internet competition, one of the most flourishing business is second hand stores. Such stores as Goodwill Industries, Thrift Shops and 2nd Avenue Value stores are teeming with shoppers. They employ many and are obviously making a profit.

Lately, when I go to Jamaica, I collect and take a whole suitcase of used clothing back to give to charity. I lug this clothing from the airport to my hotel, then I seek out a nearby charity and then lug the clothing there. Getting donations to a charity can be a pain and if made easier would encourage much more giving. Lots of Jamaicans, like me, come home for vacation. With the proper publicity, lots more Jamaicans could be persuaded to give if the process were simpler. I suggest the Jamaica Business

Corporation set up donations right in the airport. Nothing could be simpler.

I recognize distribution can be a problem. Disaster relief after a hurricane often ends up stockpiled on the pier unused. So, the solution for all these donations is setting up second hand shops with the proceeds going to charities. They will provide employment and good money for worthwhile causes instead of gathering dust at some wharf or ending up in some dump.

Miscellaneous Businesses

There are many other business in which the JGC could participate. Some of these include:

- **Maid Service Business**
  A new business that is quietly sweeping America is the maid service cleaning business. I think it would do pretty good in Jamaica too. It is the cleaning of homes and office buildings. The maids are fully trained by the company and the company guarantees results. The maids work in at least pairs. The company provides transportation, cleaning equipment and supplies for the maids. The business is bonded and insured against theft. There are fixed hourly rates and offer daily, weekly, bi-weekly service.

- **Banking Services**
  Bank of Jamaica should offer banking services to compete with banks like Nova Scotia and Barclays

with island-wide branches located in and offered as extended services of post offices.

- **Garden Service Business**
  – similar to the maid services business.
- **Jamaica Bed &Breakfast (B&B) Business** - modeled after Air B&B

CHAPTER 4

Ganja is the Way/ There is Gold in Ganja

Ganja is one of the ways to a Jamaica poor no more. Peter Tosh was right when he sang, "Legalize it". For, one of the greatest opportunities for Jamaica Government Corporation (JGC) to make a lot of money is to get into the marijuana business. Jamaica has spent great sums of money and resources trying to stamp it out. Now, ganja might be Jamaica's deliverance, deliverance from poverty. Not just by taxation but the JGC needs to obtain the maximum income from ganja by becoming directly involved in every aspect of the gamja business. The best way is to form some sort of partnership with one or both outstanding cannabis companies already in Jamaica.

Marijuana's scientific name is cannabis but it is 'ganja" to us in Jamaica. Other local names are kaya, herb and weed, but just not weed, but the "wisdom weed". Jamaica passed the "Ganja Law" in 2015 legalizing cannabis for medical or therapeutic purposes. Other countries that have legalized the medical use of cannabis include Australia, Chile, Colombia, Cyprus, Finland, Germany, Germany, Greece, Israel, Italy, Canada, Norway, the Netherlands, New Zealand, Peru, Poland, and Thailand. In the US, the medical use of cannabis is legal (with a doctor's recommendation) in 33 states, plus the District of Columbia, and the territories of Guam, Puerto Rico, the Northern Mariana Islands, and the U.S. Virgin Islands

Uruguay and Canada are the only sovereign states (as of 2018) that have fully legalized the consumption and sale of recreational cannabis nationwide. In the US, the recreational use of cannabis is legal in ten states Alaska, California, Colorado, Maine, Massachusetts, Michigan, Nevada, Oregon, Vermont, and Washington), the District of Columbia, and the Northern Mariana Islands. Another thirteen states plus the U.S. Virgin Islands have decriminalized it. Everywhere that ganja has been legalized has resulted in a financial bonanza. In the US for example, marijuana tax collections in Colorado and Washington have exceeded initial estimates, and a nationwide legalization-and-tax regime could see states raise billions of dollars per year in marijuana tax revenue. Legalizing marijuana beyond individual state to the federal level could result in an additional US$105.6 billion between 2017 and 2025, according to a report from the cannabis analytics firm New Frontier. Besides, , an analysis from the Marijuana Policy Group (MPG) showed that the legal weed created 18,005 full-time jobs and added about US$2.4 billion to Colorado's economy in 2017

The quality of our Jamaican marijuana is rated among the best in the world, both medical and recreational. Two Canadian companies were among the first to receive shipments of Jamaican marijuana.

The first, CanaQuest Medical Corp, a Canadian developer of cannabis- infused health products and pharmaceuticals, signed a preliminary agreement with Jamaican Medical Cannabis Corporation (JMCC) to provide processing, packaging, warehousing and global distribution services for CanaQuest in Jamaica. JMCC is a Toronto-headquartered company, with rapidly expanding cannabis cultivation, processing, and distribution operations in Jamaica. Its ganja farms in Jamaica encompasses a total cultivation for the company of one million square feet or 23 acres of high-quality Jamaican medical cannabis as of 2019..

The other Canadian company to receive shipments of Jamaican ganja is Synfine Research. Synfire Research is an affiliate of Toronto Research Chemicals (TRC) – both licensed dealers with Health Canada. SynFine Research, Limited has been servicing customers in over 30 countries. Synfine hopes to combine its catalog of more than 800 cannabis compounds with natural marijuana strains from Jamaica to develop products and verify their medical efficacy through clinical trials.

These Canadian companies signed these agreements to ensure a source of high-quality raw material to support CanaQuests' ongoing research programs with two prominent Canadian universities. These research programs sought to launch product formulations derived from research conducted at London, Ontario-based Western University, led by Dr Steven Laviolette. According to the company, Dr Laviolette and his team are global leaders in research for more effective use of medical cannabis for mental health.

They have identified safer and clinically superior cannabinoid formulations aimed at treating the symptoms of various psychiatric disorders such as anxiety, depression, schizophrenia, and post-traumatic stress disorder, while eliminating the negative side effects associated with traditional marijuana formats," the company said.

This sounds like a great deal. But, for the Canadian companies and Canada. They get our ganja and we get peanuts. Why ship these relatively raw ganja products and ganja itself so that other countries can do the research and development? That is more Jamaica-poor-forever policy which will deprive Jamaica of good jobs and vast sums of money. In other words such a policy is "boxing bread outta Jamaica mouth". Many people believe that this is too complex an undertaking for Jamaica. That is insulting colonial-mentality thinking. Can Jamaica undertake such a complex undertaking or shall we be just waiters, hotel maids, construction workers, "hewers of wood and drawers of water"? We are capable of doing those highly skilled jobs right here in Jamaica.

Exporting ganja leaves is not the way to go even for recreational purposes. Havana does not export tobacco leaves. Havana rolls its tobacco leaves into cigars. I, myself, have seen a single Havana cigar sell for US$75! Jamaica should not be exporting ganja leaves. Instead we should be rolling those leaves in a Jamaican factory and exporting them as finished value-added spliffs, yes Jamaican spliffs. Spliff is the Jamaican term for a hand-rolled marijuana cigarette) Who the heck rolls their own cigarettes or cigars today?   Exporting raw materials is a Jamaica-poor-forever policy. Instead we should set up factories, put Jamaicans to work expanding and creating ganja products. And not just spliffs! There are ganja infused drinks, ganja cookies and so on.

Jamaica has legalized recreational marijuana but that is not enough. We must seek out all the financial benefits that this change can produce. For instance, we should expand our tourism business by offering venues, convenient for tourists especially, where they can relax , grab a drink or coffee and enjoy smoking spliffs in luxurious surroundings. In America, there are numerous vaping lounges, where customers can relax and smoke their electronic cigarettes.

I should point out that the University of the West Indies in Jamaica has been doing research on cannabis for over ten years with great results.

Right here in Jamaica we already have our own world renowned experts on medical marijuana like Dr. Henry Lowe. Such a person is perfect for the Jamaica Business Corporation to seek out as a partner in expanding medical marijuana to its full potential in Jamaica. Dr. Lowe has successfully linked scientific research and entrepreneurship. Dr. Lowe is the Executive Chairman of the Eden Gardens Group of Companies, which specialises in health and wellness. He is also executive chairman of the Jamaican firm Medicanja. The Jamaica Health Ministry has approved at least thirteen of his cannabis extract products - a combination of topical applications, creams, spray and rubs which intended primarily to provide immediate and lasting pain relief.

Dr Lowe's prowess is international. He is a member of the prestigious American Association of Cancer Research and a life member of the New York Academy of Sciences. He has been honored by both the US House of Representatives and the New York State Senate for researching plants indigenous to Jamaica for their bioactive properties, as well as their potential for pharmaceuticals, nutraceuticals and cosmeceuticals. The New York State House also hailed him for sharing his work with other scientists and the public through published articles, reports and books.

But Dr. Lowe is not alone for outstanding Jamaican in the field of cannabis. Another visionary Jamaican pioneer in the cannabis business is Balram Vaswani.

Vaswani has worked in banking, managed Jamaica's pioneering TV network Reggae Entertainment and established the Marley Estate's coffee brand in the United States. Vaswani moved from Kingston to cash in on coffee in Denver, Colorado, but soon segued into ganja, when it became legal in that US state.

Having learned a great deal about the industrial cultivation and extraction of cannabis in Colorado, he was keen to lend his expertise to his native Jamaica, when the government announced limited research trials in partnership with two Jamaican universities. The University of the West Indies (UWI) and the University of Technology (UTech) Kingston, Jamaica.

In 2015, Vaswani set up Ganja Labs LLC, which grew legal marijuana at (UTech) under the UTech Medical Marijuana research license. Ganja Labs spent US$500,000 (J$64 million) to build out that operation, under which it launched cultivation of marijuana using three methods: indoors in temperature-controlled rooms; outdoors in smart pots exposed; and in a greenhouse, grown in an enclosed shed with natural light.

He established a place called Kaya Farms, which is located in St. Ann, right along the north coast. It was the nation's first medical marijuana complex. The facility, features a variety of attractions geared toward the promotion of cannabis wellness. All plants are organic and locally grown mixing ancient knowledge with the most innovative techniques to make sure their Ganja has a level of quality and standard on par with the best in the world.

It is also home to the Kaya Herbhouse, Kaya Spa, Kaya Café and Kaya Tours. Kaya Cafe serves ganja infused coffee and an array of juices. Of course it has smoking rooms available so that patrons relax in a pleasant atmosphere. Since then, he has set up another similar establishment in Trelawny with plans to open six more.
It is very fortunate that both Dr. Lowe and Mr. Vaswani are strong Jamaican patriots. Otherwise they could have sold off their companies to greedy avaricious multinational corporations. Doctor Lowe has acknowledge that foreign investors have tried to woo him. Vaswani also disclosed that his company has been offered several opportunities to partner with a variety of licensed holders in Canada, Australia, Israel, Hawaii and India, jurisdictions in which marijuana has been either legalised or decriminalised.. I consider that to submit to these foreign countries would be a disaster especially for medical marijuana. This could open the door to domination of the industry by Big Pharma. The effect of these big medical corporations, aka Big Pharma, is catastrophic in America. The health of Americans are held hostage so that Big Pharma can make gigantic profits. For example in America:
The EpiPen is an auto-injection system that provides a dose of epinephrine to ward off anaphylactic shock that can occur during an allergic reaction and can be fatal. The pharmaceutical company that owns EpiPen, reportedly reaped in nearly $300 million in compensation from 2011 to 2015. This massive profits arose because the list prices for EpiPens soared, increasing over 500% in about a decade. Today, EpiPens, which cost the drug company around $30 to produce, go for over $600 before coupons or rebates.

Another price-gouging in America by Big Pharma is about insulin which is used to treat diabetes. Insulin prices have been rising so much that some diabetics are spending as much on monthly diabetes-related expenses as their mortgage payment. Without their daily insulin injection, the 1.25 million Americans with diabetes could fall into a coma or even die. It's led some people living with diabetes to turn to the black market, crowdfunding pages, and Facebook pages to get access to the life-saving drug. Some others turn to Mexico. Fortunately, Mexican pharmacies can offer price relief. In a price survey conducted in April of 2017, it was found that three types of insulin that are sold across the border at a discount pharmacy in Nogales, Mexico for $50 a vial. Those same medications were sold in the US at a typical price" of between $385 and $538 a vial. Some others just die.

Don't let Big Pharma get hold of Jamaican cannabis. Instead the Jamaica Government Corporation should seek to become partners with both Jamaican companies or at least one of them. This ensuing union will expand Jamaica's cannabis industry at home and abroad for the benefit of all Jamaicans. But such a union is a relatively new concept and the choice of the CEO of the Jamaica Business Corporation is crucial to success.

Balram Vaswani as JGC CEO

I think the perfect person to take up this challenge is Mr. Balram Vaswani, the CEO of Kaya. Mr. Vaswani has a distinguished background as a businessman. Since JGC would be running multiple businesses, not ganja alone,
Mr. Vaswani impressive credentials include:
- experience in banking,
- pioneering Jamaica's TV network Reggae Entertainment
- CEO of Marley Coffee in Jamaica (2009-2014,2017)

•   helping to establish Marley Coffee in Denver, along with Rohan Marley, the son of Bob Marley

•   His foresight in moving to Denver to get in on the groundfloor of the burgeoning ganja business there

•   He demonstrated big ideas for cannabis forming such a comprehensive business with announced plans to set up up as many as eight Kaya herbhouses across Jamaica. So far, he has set up two, one in St. Ann and one in Trelawny.

•   His sensitivity in giving credit and respect to the Rastas for the fight, cruelty endured and endurance in their defence of ganja over the years.

•   His patriotism and pride in Jamaica

•   He had former Jamaica prime minister P J Patterson on the board of directors for Kaya Inc..

There might be concern whether he might be able to handle the job since he is already the CEO of Kaya Inc.. However, there is precedent when super Jamaican hotelier Butch Stewart took over Air Jamaica, although he was still CEO of the Sandals hotels empire. Sadly, even his excellent business skills could not save Air Jamaica and it joined the graveyard like so many other airlines all over the world.

Clearly, Mr. Vaswani is the man for such an innovative and challenging job as CEO of JGC. But, will he take the job?

Chapter 5

Introducing Partnership With People - the Solution to the Economic Crisis

Letter on PWP to Caribbean Officials
The following letter was sent to selected Caribbean Officials in October 1998 along with the article "Introducing PWP". The letter is as follows:)

Dear (Caribbean Official),
I remain deeply concerned about the economic plight of my native Jamaica, the Caribbean and all other developing countries. I am alarmed at the current policies such as the IMF structural adjustment, globalisation, "free trade", privatisation, which all make rich powerful multinational corporations even more rich and powerful, and leave countries politically weaker and so far with no positive economic benefits to show for all this. I am proposing something new for Government to follow, which I am confident will lead to real prosperity and regain or retain our country from insensitive multinational corporations.

I have attached some brief characteristics of this program, which I call Partnership With People (PWP). Please give it serious consideration and do not ignore it because of its seemingly overly optimistic goals. I am sending this package to other Caribbean officials, including Heads-of-State. I would be glad to discuss it with you and so address any questions or provide further details.

I have also included a copy of the October issue of Hot Calaloo newsletter. An article in it, "Whither...IMF Privatisation or PWP Prosperity?" In this article I set the stage to introduce PWP. I have been the editor/producer of Hot Calaloo from 1992. The Hot Calaloo web page is located at: http://www.dclink.com/hcal/index.htm (since moved to **http://gonow.to/hotcalaloo***)*

I do not intend to publish the description of PWP in the newsletter or on the Web until I give you and the other Caribbean officials a chance to respond. Also, I have to consider whether such details might be better withheld now to keep it from enemies of the Caribbean.

I look forward to hearing from you.

Keep looking. Answer came there none.

Enough is Enough

In Jamaica like most of the world, the economic "salvation" was imported. Privatisation, globalisation, IMF imposed structural adjustment, currency liberalization, free trade, etc. have failed. How much longer shall we pursue these policies before our leaders realize this? Unfortunately, our leaders may be powerless to change course. Even in their own countries, they have no say. The fact is these policies have undermined the economic sovereignty of our countries to international organisations like the IMF, the World Trade Organisations (WTO), the World Bank, etc. These organisations are dominated by big rich countries and multinational corporations. Right now the WTO has imperiled the Jamaica banana trade with the European Union.

Consequences

In Jamaica the failure of these policies are so evident as shown by:

- banks have been dropping like flies
- the dairy industry recently had to dump 76,000 liters of milk partly due to cheap imported powdered milk

- the privatised sugar industry collapsed under millions of dollars in debt and fell back into Government hands
- the beef industry were forced into public protest at McDonalds which buys only imported beef because it is cheaper by 14 cents per pound.
- the Jamaica cement company is millions of dollars in debt as cheaper imported cement makes big inroads into the local Jamaica market
- farmers in the parish of St. Elizabeth leave their abundant crops unharvested because they cannot compete with cheaper imports
- the banana companies have restructured into one Agris Services company to be more competitive with the "Dollar" bananas of multinational US corporations led by Chiquita. Every worker was made redundant and the new company rehired about 2000 of them, but at lower wages and decreased benefits. The workers are not happy but "glad to have a job".
- these "Dollar" bananas are so much cheaper than the local ones, if they were imported into Jamaica, would wipe out the Jamaica banana industry. So we could not only lose the EU market, but even our own local market

For Whose benefit?
Who is benefitting from these policies? Not the people of Jamaica. But, multinational corporations, like Chiquita, are. Not only here, but all over the world, even in NAFTA countries. They bear down on the local industry, driving them into bankruptcy, like a Wallmart up against a mom-and-pop store in the US. Privatisation, globalisation, free trade...they all play into the hands of multinational corporations.

Partnership With People (PWP) - the Way to Prosperity

Still the IMF is calling for more aggressive privatisation for Jamaica and most other struggling countries. This privatisation is a bound-to-fail policy. Governments end up selling off their money-making entities, for which there is demand, and get stuck with the money-losing ones. This is a clear formula for failure. If it were the other way around, then I would be an enthusiastic supporter. But this privatisation is not the only game in town. I am proposing a new game, Partnership With People (PWP). PWP will not only bring prosperity, but has the potential to restore the country to its people and from the clutches of powerful insensitive multinational corporations.

Introducing Partnership With People (PWP)

The Government will set up PWP corporation. PWP will in turn form subsidiary corporations specifically to provide goods or services at a profit. These PWP corporations would be relatively autonomous but under the umbrella of PWP. Some features of these PWP corporations will include:

- -extensive feasibility study to ensure profitability potential
- obtain marketing and other technical expertise on short term contract
- -take advantage of Govt contacts and access
- - determine formula for success by comparison with similar corporations not only in Jamaica but worldwide
- - this formula will then be followed rigidly
- -PWP would run the corporation for a limited time to ensure profitably and high standards

- -PWP would then sell the enterprise to private individuals, partners, but maintain control by an iron-clad contract which would spell out very rigid terms such as:
- -the name (Trademark) of the enterprise could not be changed
- - sale to a partner would be in the form of a down payment with a % of sales coming to PWP in perpetuity or for some defined period.
- -PWP would control management style deciding such fundamentals as training standards and salary of employees
- -PWP would provide advertising, and state of the art professional marketing and management
- -Supplies would be bought only from PWP sources
- -Buildings would have to be maintained according to PWP standards with no changes without PWP authorization
- -Since PWP policies and management techniques are obtained from established successful companies, failure to follow to the letter would void the contract and the private partner could even lose the enterprise and forfeit their deposit. This is a vital aspect of this plan as it depends on following what works, and models like these have a greater than 90% success rate.

An important aspect of PWP is that, since unlike other Govt. operations, this one is for profit. Employees salary would depend on the profits of PWP. Basically, the bigger the profits, the better the pay. Given a certain time to turn a profit, PWP should not only pay for itself but provide revenues to the Government.

In a nutshell, PWP is a franchise operation in which the Government is the franchiser and private individuals, partners, would be franchisees. Currently franchises are very expensive, making it difficult to find partners. So, creative financing. substituting products and services for financing, manipulation of fees and royalties, and such flexibility might have to be used to ensure supply of partners, each with a real stake in the business.

Background

Recently I was in France. There, I obtained a map of Paris. The map was free and produced by the McDonalds Fast food corporation. There were little golden arches all over the map, each indicating where a McDonalds was located. I thought something was wrong with that picture. Well PWP will fix that picture without doing like Bermuda, which banned McDonalds from that country.

Franchises are everywhere for everything here in the US, from Kwick Copy printing shops, maid service, Post Office boxes....everything. Besides they have a greater than 90% success rate and soon I predict they will be sweeping the Caribbean. All that money leaving the Caribbean, unless PWP is launched......

Success

Back to McDonalds... A very good friend of mine, a fellow Jamaican, attended high school here in the US. He then went to college, my alma mater, Howard University. Upon graduation, he went to England and became a barrister. He then returned to Jamaica. About four years later, he threw in the towel, abandoned Jamaica, and returned to the US. A barrister in the US! Worthless. In a few months I heard he had exchanged his legal wig for an apron and had become a manager at McDonalds. Now, years later, he has two McDonalds franchises and is wealthy!

The Challenge
The immediate challenge is can the Government successfully set up its own franchises? Now is the time to find out before we have to compete with more multinational corporations coming in and taking the bread out of our mouths. There are lots of information and expert consultants on franchising. We do not have to re-invent the wheel. A visit to the Internet will show a wealth of information on all sorts of franchises. Ben and Jerry Ice Cream deserves special mention and real consideration as a model. They are a franchise corporation with a social conscience and proves that this is not incompatible with profit. Their highest paid employee up till recently by policy made no more than eight times the lowest paid employee. Of course, this ratio is probably too low to attract partners, but it shows how this can be an incredibly fair and equitable system. *"Yes Virginia...we can use the incentive of the profit motive, but without the contamination by greed."*

Sources of PWP Franchises

- Government Divestment - instead of the traditional privatising, each enterprise should be evaluated for PWP feasibility, and adopted if prospects for profits look good.
- Existing successful private enterprises - Historically, franchises usually have started out as a single business. With success, the operations are then spread by franchise to other areas, even internationally. In this instance, PWP will look at certain successful private enterprises in the country, evaluate their feasibility for PWP, and if good, invite the owners to expand via PWP. So branches might open up in other areas all over the country. This way

ensures a proven product, and an expert partner (the owner), who would derive additional benefits for his or her expertise and extra managerial duties for each additional store.

- Existing struggling private enterprises - Some business are struggling because they need professional management, capital investment, and/or better organisation. PWP could seek out such businesses, invite owners to join, and reorganise them professionally under PWP guidelines and terms.
- Create brand new enterprises - Instead of waiting for private sector, Government would set up a profitable business to fulfill some need in the community, establish its profitability and value, then turn it over to PWP. As they say, the way to entrepreneurial success is to "find a need and fill it".
- Also, private individual could identify a business potential, for which he needs help to set up. He could then convince the Government to set it up as a PWP project with him as the partner if he or she qualifies.

The Choice

Recently I saw in the Jamaican papers much fanfare about the opening of a Century 21 Real Estate office in Jamaica. More franchise profits to a foreign company and also getting free advertising advantage over our own Jamaican real estate companies! While in France, I received a map of Pariswith a slew of MacDonalds identified all over the city. This represented roads of money leading back to McDonald corporation! These multinational corporations are coming and it will be "join them or go out of business". We'll become like the little stores in the US when a WalMart comes in the area, they all die! These franchisers do provide excellent management, but they all follow a proven formula. In this information age,

PWP too can follow that formula, elevate the level of service and business standards extensively, make money for our partners and the Government, and rescue our country from rich multinational corporations. PWP is flexible too as it can decide what operations to undertake, and the rate at which to spread these operations. It can select the more feasible. PWP and invite partners to join it without forcing anyone. Critics might contend that PWP is not new. To be sure, franchising is not new, which is good, because it has an established record of success. But, PWP is a new role for Government. The choice is clear. Is it the enfranchisement of our people by PWP or our continued disenfranchisement by rich multinational corporations? The choice has got to be PWP or at least it deserves a try!

Chapter 6

Proposed PWP Operations

(These proposals are from the originals published in Hot Calaloo in 1998-99)

FINSAC, PWP and Port Antonio
(from Hot Calaloo, V 7#4, Dec 1998)

The Jamaica Government formed the FINSAC corporation in order to rescue not government but private institutions such as banks and insurance companies, the pillars of private enterprise. It monitors these institutions, determines their financial health, rescue them from bankruptcy, put them back in a healthy financial condition, establishes rules of operation, and then sells them back to some other private sector company or investor. In order to accomplish so complex an operation it hires its expertise usually at great expense. It is in the red, running up huge debts, but economic catastrophe and the loss of public confidence have been averted. So, despite the price tag, it has to be considered a success.

There are lots of similarities with the FINSAC operation and the Partnership With People (PWP), the concept proposed by Hot Calaloo. PWP, an autonomous government corporation, undertakes to run private enterprise operation with private sector partners. PWP hires expertise to run the operation. It investigates the operation for profitability potential. It establishes the rules of operation. It monitors it for efficiency and professionalism. PWP is designed to make a profit, not a rescue operation, like FINSAC, so would select only operations that have profit potential. A reader raised a good question as to whether PWP would compete and displace some small struggling entrepreneur. It might, but so too would some big multinational chain operation if it could make a profit in so doing. At least PWP would consider this impact, ways to minimize this, and even invite the local entrepreneur to be a partner.

On my recent trip to Port Antonio, it was precisely this struggling entrepeneur that I saw many signs of how PWP could help.Here are three examples.

Hotel

I had lunch in this hotel high in the mountains of Port Antonio. It had an impressive spectacular view, the best in the area by far. But, that was all it had. Once a mecca in its heyday many years ago, it was now antiquated. The rooms were deplorable and I was told that it seldom had any guests. How it stayed afloat was a mystery. Maids, attendants, cooks, waiters and the rest of the hotel staff would lose their jobs if the hotel closes. It would be a tragedy. I am sure PWP could save it. They could remodel, advertising blitz, establish shuttle to the beach, aggressive campaign to make it up to date and competitive and restore it to its former glory. At the least, PWP would obtain the expertise to make it financially sound. Or, shall we wait for Holiday Inn or some other financial multinational corporation, or bankruptcy?

Horseback Riding

I encountered a local resident struggling to make a go of horseback riding for tourists. This would be a real easy project for PWP. All it would take would be providing a cell phone, riding helmets, good advertising in the hotels, and some minimal training in running a business in a professional manner. Some additional horses would be good to accomodate the increase in business that would result.

Reach Falls Shop

I went to the beautiful Reach Falls. At the entrance I bought some delicious shrimp tea (soup) loaded with big tasty crayfish. It was dispensed from a ramshackle stall that many a tourist would probably avoid. There were other local vendors selling ital tonics etc. A nice inexpensive attractive even shed-like building plus some PWP business counseling would be a tremendous boost to the sales of these vendors.

In all of these ventures, PWP would invite these people to be partners. It would be voluntary. PWP could actually investigate the feasibility in advance and propose to accept payment for their services as a percentage of the increase in net profits above what the present owners are making now. PWP could easily become a pro-active extension of FINSAC.

Fixing the Markets the PWP Way
(from Hot Calaloo, V 7#4, Dec 1998)

"Carry me ackee
go ah Linstead Market
Not a quattie wut sell...."

"Come we go down
Come we go down
Come we go down
Ah Solas market.."

Market day in Jamaica is a big event in the lives of many, especially in the countryside. But, reports indicate the markets are deteriorating . In Mandeville vendors are refusing to use the market there because it is so filthy, choosing to occupy sidewalks instead. Here, they become targets of police who need to keep the sidewalks clear. The same type of thing is true for even crafts market. Recently Ocho Rios crafts market vendors staged a series of demonstrations because their potential customers, tourists were avoiding these markets like the plague. And why not? These craft markets are

- unattractive
- often dirty
- contain a glut of the same products
- filled with desperate vendors who often resort to techniques just short of harassment to sell their products

The PWP Solution

First of all, the markets should be run on professional market principles. The poor vendors know nothing about this so the Government will have to both establish and teach them. There is a desperate need and only Government can fill it. In the Partnership with People (PWP) way, Government would appoint a market CEO, whose salary would be dependent on the financial success of the market. The market would be run on business and marketing principles like shopping malls in the US. The CEO would run the market with input from a board of directors. This board of directors would be comprised of the vendors, or selected or elected members from and representing all the vendors. To begin with toilet facilities would be stocked and maintained by an attendant. The CEO and board would constantly seek to:

- Establish and maintain cleanliness
- provide good security
- increase patronage
- minimize harassment
- improve quality
- seek solutions to any other problems that arises.

Vendors would probably have to pay more but not be restricted to cash only, but maybe in percentage of sales, goods, or their labour to maintain the market. New rules would define each vending site location and area. Vendors would not only have additional responsibility in keeping their vending site and a specified adjacent area clean, but would have to participate in other aspects of the running of the market, like serving on the board. Markets have to be saved and the PWP way (*described only briefly*) can transform these awful dirty warehouses into attractive pleasant retail outlets to which shoppers will want to come. Increased sales will result and increased profit as well as the development of business skills for the vendors. Besides, just as shopping malls make a profit, the Government too should also make a profit out of this partnership, which would be a nice bonus.

Making Petrojam Flourish by PWP

(from Hot Calaloo, V 7#5, Jan 1999)

So far the Government of Jamaica has been unable to divest itself of its petroleum refinery. This might be a good thing as it provides an opportunity for a perfect PWP, Partnership With People, project

Partnership With People (PWP) is Hot Calaloo's proposed autonomous government corporation responsible for seeking out, establishing, obtaining partners for, and maintaining franchise operations for a wide variety of goods and services.

Petrojam refinery produces all gasolene sold in Jamaica, be it Exon, Shell or Texaco. Instead this proposal would create PWP's Petrojam gas stations. But these would not be just gas stations. Just as the new proposed postal centers would incorporate an array of new services, so also would the new

Petrojam stations. They would be modeled after the gas station-convenience stores now quite popular here in the USA. So these gas stations would become little retail centers of goods and services in which they would :

- Sell gas
- Sell selected auto supplies
- Sell groceries
- Sell snacks such as patties, sodas etc. (cold supper shop)
- Do auto repairs

This Petrojam station would be set up as a PWP franchise. PWP would be responsible for obtaining management expertise to ensure high quality. They would be responsible for :

- staff training
- service
- competence
- cleanliness
- professionalism
- advertising
- bookkeeping and accounting
- policies
- security

Partners or Franchisees

Each Petrojam station would operate as a co-operative and may have as many as four franchisees.

- One for selling gas and auto supplies
- One for auto repair shop
- One for selling groceries
- One for selling snacks

PWP would try to get franchisees already operating similar enterprises in the area. Every attempt would be made not to compete and displace these existing entrepreneurs, but to incorporate them in a more professional and of course profitable venture.

This will be a shining glistening place with courteous well-trained efficient motivated staff. It will be a hub of activity.

I am convinced PWP is not just a way out of poverty for Jamaica and the rest of the Caribbean, but a blueprint for prosperity, and a means to recapture our economic sovereignty.

Chapter 7

The Root of All Evil

Jamaicanism will reduce poverty in Jamaica but unless she rejects the money-hogging rat race culture, there will not sufficient improvement in the quality of life.

Jamaica, like most countries worldwide, is affected by a pervasive addiction which has corrupted the living environment. Jamaica is smaller, so it's more noticeable there. It is the evil created by the addiction to money and power. The love of money is the root of all evil and Jamaica is no exception. Out of this lust for money, societies have become a money-hogging materialistic rat race. The characteristics of the money- hogging, materialistic rat race are: riches, poverty, selfishness, discontent, inequality, belligerence, waste, extravagance, insensitivity, luxury, ostentation, vanity, snobbery, exploitation, deceit and even war.

The supreme prize for winning the rat race is money, lots of money. Rat race societies are driven by our love of money or what Pope Francis calls, ***"The idolatry of money"***. We have been addicted to money. It is an addiction worse than drugs. Just as drug lords and drug pushers increase their wealth and power by spreading the addiction, the money lords and money pushers do likewise. However, drug lords and drug pushers must do their evil deeds in the dark corners, abandoned buildings, in the sinister shadowy furtive places. But, money lords and money pushers ply their trade in the open by seductive unrelenting advertising. Drug lords and drug pushers are reviled but money lords and money pushers are revered. They are so revered that they become the leaders and role models for society.

Addiction

The rat race has driven us to become money-materialism addicts. Addiction is slavery. Many, because of addiction to drugs, alcohol, gambling, etc., have lost their jobs, families, friends and ended up in the gutter. Such is the nature of addiction and that is what restoring the goodness of man is up against. We lose the freedom to choose. We are driven. It ruins the quality of life. Some abandon family for it. It allows us to be manipulated. Up the price and we go along. Addiction is a curse. It invades the addicts life and takes control of it. It is destructive.

The Addict

The rat race has so conditioned us to money as the universal goal and key to happiness in life that money has become a sacred cow. So, money is unchallenged and accepted as the "normal" goal of life. But, we do not realize that we are just addicts to money, wanting more and more and never being satisfied, never having enough. The things people do for money!
It is for this love of money that some :

- Kill for it
- Steal for it
- Mug for it
- Invade countries for it
- Bomb innocents for it
- Cheat for it
- Intimidate for it
- Lie for it
- Ruin reputation for it
- Sell their souls for it

We are driven by consumer mania and manipulated by advertising. We are so brainwashed that it is very difficult to break this addiction. All addiction is difficult to break, but even acknowledging this money mania as addiction is difficult. Instead we are told this lust for money is good. It shows we are ambitious, want to get ahead and receives all sorts of praise in our society.

The Pushers
The pushers, these money lords, enrich themselves at the expense of their victims, the addicts. It is the source of their power, so they have a vested interest in keeping us addicted and will fight to protect their turf. Pushers control your life. They have you running all over the place like a chicken with its head cut-off trying to feed your addiction.

The worst consequences – crime, political corruption and division
Even if Jamaica reduces poverty substantially, the quality of life will not improve sufficiently as long as the money-hogging rat race dominates our culture. But this addiction is curable. The first step in addiction is to choke off the demand, this insatiable demand for more and more money, this voracious materialism. It has overvalued money and devalued people. When we devalue people we make relationships with people unimportant. Relationships are the social glue that holds our society together. So all relationships, such as family relationships and friendships, become unimportant and deteriorate.

The 3 M's: Money, Materialism, Meanness
If money and materialism are the way to happiness, then poor people will always be the unhappiest people in the land. If the attainment of riches and wealth is the way to happiness, then poor people will never be happy. Fortunately it is not, but most of us have been brainwashed into thinking so.

Buy to impress!
But let us not kid ourselves. We have been so brainwashed that rejecting this universal goal of the love for money is not easy. In our money-oriented society we must deal with the siren song of advertisers. This new form of slavery is

voluntary mental slavery due to the brainwashing of advertisers. As Bob Marley sings the words of Marcus Garvey, we will have to *"free ourselves from mental slavery, none but ourselves can free our minds"*.

Even among the poorest, who virtually have no money and don't stand much chance of getting any, advertisers crawl inside their heads and keep telling them to buy, buy, buy.

"Yes master. I hear and I will obey. I will go out and buy an overpriced, gas-guzzling, environment –depleting, ugly, huge, non-streamlined, overturn-prone, 4-wheeled drive SUV capable of climbing Mount Everest in a blizzard. I hea, master and I will obey. I will obey…I will obey……"

Resist! Don't fall for all that rat race buy propaganda. Buy smart instead.

Abuse of Power

The rat race has also created a lust for power. The more money we have, the more power we have. So, just as we crave material things, we also crave power. Now power itself is not bad. Parents need power to raise their children properly. It is a necessary part of society. But, remember power corrupts and absolute power corrupts absolutely But money is not the only source of power. Give a man a gun, he has power. Promote a man to be boss, he has power. Make a man a cop, a president, he has power.

The lust for power is one of the products of the money-hogging rat race. Unfortunately, some misuse or even abuse of power is an acceptable cultural norm. This widespread misuse and abuse of power is one of the most serious problems our society faces, which is even more critical because it is not recognized as such. Everywhere merit takes a backseat to power. It pervades almost every aspect of our lives. It is of epidemic proportions.

Some proponents include:
- Police
- Spouses

- Bosses
- Politicians
- Bullies
- Gangs
- Employers

It produces:
- Racism
- Class discrimination
- Police brutality
- Extortion
- Inefficiency
- Victimisation
- Wars
- Exploitation

Unfortunately, our rat race society is replete with the abuse of power. Power is used to bully and exploit. Schoolyard bullies grow up to be perpetrators of domestic violence and other types of social misfits. Too many lust for power. Marriages disintegrate as spouses battle for power.

The fact is we have constant power struggles in all aspects of life, not just marriages. We have power struggles in, our jobs, our organisations, politics, between countries. You name it. These undermine relationships and threaten our ability to work together.
Conversely, the less power you have, the more you are likely to be pushed around and abused. Black people in the ghetto in the USA are powerless, are pushed around and are subject to abuse. They have no money, so, some get power by getting a gun or joining a gang.
However, let us not forget that one of the most powerful men in the world had neither wealth nor did he wield a gun.

He derived his power from doing good, from being good. I speak of Dr. Martin Luther King Jr..

Resist

To create the magnificent society in Jamaica, we must resist this buying mania. It is not easy. That buy-propaganda is strong stuff. We are up against a rich and powerful brainwashing advertising industry. This advertising industry have employed psychologists, psychiatrists, marketing experts, and all sorts of head experts at big bucks for the sole purpose of getting into our heads to distort our thinking in order to buy their unwanted products. In our present culture:

- We must buy to impress friends.
- We must buy to prove that we are worthy human beings.
- We must buy these un-needed products or our spouses or lovers might leave us and some indeed will.

If you do not buy ,this society will think you are one of the poor and wretched of the earth and despise you. So many poor people cannot afford to buy these but feel driven to acquire them by hook or crook in order to disguise their poverty.

Surplus Money

To reject money and materialism does not mean going without money. We need money to live. We need money to satisfy our basic needs. We need money to live comfortably. The rich have more money than needed to satisfy their needs. So, they have surplus money. The poor do not have enough money to satisfy their needs. The problem is that worldwide, the rich are getting richer and the poor are getting poorer. This means the rich are getting more surplus money while the poor are getting less money to meet their basic needs. That does not seem fair.

Money for basic needs includes at least food, housing, clothing education, and health care. Money to live comfortably is not as straightforward. It actually depends on our culture. Our prevailing money-hogging culture demands we go beyond comfort and acquire as great a money surplus as we can. It puts money on a pedestal. This culture generates a powerful love of money which is the root of all evil. We must reject this culture. It is time for a cultural revolution.

Chapter 8

Inherently Good

"What a piece of work is a man! How noble in reason! how infinite in faculty! in form, in moving, how express and admirable! in action how like an angel! in apprehension how like a god! the beauty of the world! the paragon of animals!"
– William Shakespeare, 'Hamlet'

Evil is very pervasive in our society and all over the world. But, this is not normal. It is an aberration. It is not normal because we are born good. We are going to restore the Jamaica back to normalcy by the Goodwill Revolution.

In South Africa, Nelson Mandela was jailed for 26 years. He witnessed the brutality and oppression of his people for decades in which they were treated like dogs, herded in their own land like cattle, denied even the status of human beings and a slew of other vicious repressions because they were black,. But they overcame it. In the words of Nelson Mandela, in his farewell speech from Parliament, *"Historical enemies succeeded in negotiating a peaceful transition from apartheid to democracy because we were prepared to accept **the inherent goodness in the other**"*. This inherent goodness of man was a source of power for this liberation and the peaceful transition of South Africa from these horrors of apartheid. Unfortunately, the money-hogging rat race undermines this inherent goodness of man, but the goodwill revolution strengthens and reinforces it. This inherent goodness is the source of power for the goodwill-to-all revolution.

Good or Bad
We are all born good. This is one of the strongest reason why the Goodwill-to-all Revolution will succeed. I know that philosophers have long pondered the nature of man. Is

he good or bad? Fundamental to the goodwill revolution is the conviction that people are inherently good.

The evidence is abundantly clear that we are all born good. Why else do we care about things like fairness and justice? We do not want justice only for our relatives and friends, we want justice for all. We do not want to see people suffer, go hungry. We would like to see all workers make at least a living wage. We don't want to see children go hungry, not just our child, but any child, Why? Because it is our nature to be good. We are inherently good. It is natural for us to care about others.

We care about people we don't know and people who don't even exist. We go to the movies and care for the plight of the make-believe hero. So, we love happy endings, because in happy endings good usually triumphs, or the homeless person gets fed, or the sick person is healed or justice prevails. We do not just want these good things in the movies, but we hunger for them in our lives. And very important, we are not selfish to want good things just for ourselves, but by our very nature, we want them for all.

Conversely, we despise and hate evil. Why? Because we are inherently good. Because we are inherently good, we hate and abhor evil. We hate and abhor the bully. We hate and abhor the abuse and exploitation of the weak and innocent. We hate and abhor murder, robbery, child molestation, kidnapping and all those vicious crimes committed against anyone, friend or foe. It is natural to hate evil acts and the people that commit them. It is natural to hate the bombing, killing and destruction of millions of men, women and children in war. It is natural for us to hate torture and human degradation.

Doing an evil deed is not just clear sailing. Before we can do it, we must contend with our basic instinct which tells us not to do it, our conscience. Conscience opposes the evil act and exerts pressure to try to prevent it. Unfortunately, conscience does not have veto power, and so it can be overcome. But even after overcoming conscience and committing the dastardly deed, human nature runs into more opposition from remorse and guilt.

After committing an evil deed, guilt is our innate goodness trying to make a breakthrough and reassert itself. But alas, these instincts for good are not indestructible and like the UN can be rendered completely irrelevant. But their very existence is another bit of evidence that mankind is inherently good.

All our institutions are based on the inherent goodness of man.

Democracy depends on the inherent goodness of man.

Justice - The jury trial is based upon the inherent goodness of man.

All the good qualities we seek such as fairness, equality, freedom, equal opportunity, and peace depend on the inherent goodness of man.

Not only is man naturally good but he wants to do good. He does not want to do evil. Evil goes against the grain. Even the robber probably does not want to rob. Even the 9-11 terrorists probably did not really want to murder those hundreds of innocent people in the World Trade Center in New York. Before or after these acts, the perpetrators are compelled to justify. In so doing, they are saying *"these horrible acts are really good because..."* Why do they have to? Because they don't want good people to despise them. They don't want good people to consider them evil. They go to great lengths to justify these evil deeds as good. So, for evil deeds to gain acceptance, they must masquerade as good. This is but another powerful reason that we are inherently good and the primacy of this good nature which must be satisfied. The bottom line is not only do we not want to do bad things, but we also do not want to be perceived as doing bad things. So I believe that Israelis and Palestinians, Hindus and Muslims, Irish Catholics and Protestants, Tutsis and Hutus, and many other bitter antagonists that imperil our world today, do not really want to kill one another. It is unnatural.

We still feel inside a sense of outrage when we see injustice, but we do nothing about it. We still feel a compassion for genuine poverty, misery and misfortune in others, but we do nothing about it. So at a movie, we are moved by a touching and moving make-believe story. This fake story might even be better than reality because we do not *have* to do anything about it. And, that's the problem, which makes us want to even deny our feelings of goodwill, or to even fight against them. We deny them and try to embrace apathy, insensitivity, because we feel helplessness to do anything about it. Why bother?

The obvious question the arises, "*If man is born good, why does evil prosper?*" Because we have created a society that has deviated from man's natural inclination for good. We have created the money-hogging rat race. We have created a society rooted in the love of money. The love of money is the root of all evil. Yes, we have s created a deviant society which has diminished man's inherent goodness for the love and addiction to money.

What ever happened to being "fair"? The rat race has pretty much killed it or at least made it pretty irrelevant. A popular phrase these days is, "*Where is it written that I need to be fair?*" How cynical! Answer is, "Here". It is written here in the goodwill revolution. It is a primary requirement of the goodwill revolution.

In the rat race, good is often a handicap. So, this natural force to do good within us is suppressed. It is relatively dormant, but it is still there waiting to be released.

Let's liberate it. We intend to establish a beachhead of the Goodwill-to-all Revolution in Jamaica.

Don't fight that feeling of goodwill. The goodwill revolution taps into that goodness of man. It is a source of power. It is that source of power which waged the greatest revolution in American history and won against tremendous odds. And I do not mean the revolution against the British. No it was a revolution that pitted ordinary people armed and united by goodwill against unjust laws, against police terror, violent mobs, even vicious dogs, a most formidable enemy indeed. It was the civil rights revolution of the sixties. White people of goodwill fought against a system that bestowed upon them a wide assortment of special privileges. White people of goodwill endured violence and insults of others of their own privileged white kith and kin to join with blacks in the fight. Black and white people of goodwill fought together against segregation. Black and white people united by goodwill died together against segregation. Black and white people of goodwill fought against a system that denied black people basic civil rights. And, they did not do it for money. On the contrary, many lost money as they lost work time, even jobs. They did not do it for prestige as many faced ostracism, ridicule and worse. No, they did not do it for these typical prizes of the rat race. They did it for their sense of justice, fairness, because of their inherent goodness, a most powerful and natural force. This is the force that will propel the goodwill revolution.

The good news is that in this new goodwill revolution, Jamaicans will not have to face the perils that the battle of the civil rights revolution in America required. Different times require different methods. This goodwill revolution will create a society that reinforces man's inherent goodness instead. We need the Goodwill-to-all Revolution. Revolution is not easy. It will be a tough battle but it will place no one at risk of any physical harm or arrest. So, for the Goodwill Revolution, nature is on our side.

.

Chapter 9

The Goodwill Revolution for Jamaica

Polarization
One of the greatest problems countries face all over the world is the polarization of its peoples. Some of these issues include, religion, race, political party, tribe, socioeconomic status, class, Look all over the world and back into history and see how these differences have ravaged and continues to ravage the world.
Some examples:

- Rohinga in Myanmar - Isis has killed thousands of its fellow Muslims, proudly showing some of these killings by gruesome public beheadings.
- Genocide in Ruwanda - In the Rwandan genocide tribal gangs of Hutu gangs killed an estimated 500,000 to 1,000,000 members of the Tutsi tribe and raped an estimated 250,000 to 500,000 women.
- Boko Harim in Nigeria - In Nigeria, Boko Haram has killed thousands and displaced 2.3 million from their homes.
- Isis in the middle East - Isis has killed thousands of its fellow Muslims, proudly showing some of these killings by gruesome public beheadings.
-

These killing do not come from invasions but they are all killing their own people.
Democracy sounds great but how many are killed come election time? It is a great system because through elections the people speak. But, they also riot, murder, cheat, intimidate. The sad fact is democracy severely polarizes people in Jamaica and all over the world. In addition:

- It is expensive
- It breeds hostility

- It is so corrosive it scares good people away from becoming candidates
- It produces politicians who as a class are disdained by people in general
- It create almost cult-like followers
- It wastes valuable resources on perpetuating itself
- It breeds corruption and favoritism

The fact is that people become so polarized that they kill each other. The goodwill revolution recognizes this problem as its objective is to create goodwill to all regardless of any kind of difference including political differences.

Sure Jamaica is not as bad as these examples, but Jamaicans are killing each other at an alarming rate. Crime, violence and political corruption are rampant. Beloved reggae icons Bob Marley was shot in Jamaica and . Peter Tosh was shot and killed in Jamaica by our own fellow Jamaicans. Jamaica was not good enough for Louise Bennett and Jimmy Cliff to retire. Our beloved Louise Bennett left Jamaica to spend her declining years abroad in Canada. Jimmy Cliff chose England. A Jamaican's home is his castle but instead of a moat for protection, he must live behind bars, burglar bars.

"The people united can never be defeated."
This is absolutely true, but, people are being defeated everywhere. Politicians have the primary task of keeping people united. Unfortunately, an effective tactic for gaining political power is by dividing people and turning them against each other. So we see these ruthless politicians like Donald Trump, use divisive tactics such as race, religion, class, national origin to gain power. He gains power over the people, but the people are defeated. We need politicians who can bring people together, politicians with goodwill for all.

So what is being done about this evil? No enough. Not
enough in the world. Not enough in Jamaica
Too often we look to America for solutions because its
culture is dominating the world. But, that culture is the
greatest proponent of the money-hogging power-seeking
rat race. They have elected a dishonest, racist liar as
president for God's sake! According to Center for Economic
and Policy Research, America has killed 40,000 innocent
Venezuelans in about six months with their sanctions in
their attempt to install their puppet as president. Such
heinous actions do not seem to raise much moral outrage
and that's a substantial part of the problem. How can we
oppose evil when so many fail to recognize it or are so
complacent?
The fact is Jamaica, with all its flaws, is far superior to the
vaunted America in the execution of democratic principles.
Money has completely undermined their system. Jamaican
politicians, both JLP and PNP, represent the people.
American politicians represent the big multi-national
corporations and the ultra- rich who fund their expensive
political campaigns.

Apathy and complacency to evil is a worldwide crisis, but, it
is business as usual. Instead we continue to promote money
and power to the status of gods. But unless we do
something about it, evil will continue to flourish. Jamaica
must break out of that mold for things could get even
worse. Jamaica must seek its own solution. We have had
some band aids but we need a whole cultural revolution.
Jamaica needs to join and lead the revolution, the Goodwill
Revolution, and show the world.
But, you probably think, "Money is so wonderful" and
frown on goodwill as sort of corny and unglamorous. Since
we are addicted to money, we are conditioned to think so. If

we break that addiction, then we will be able to appreciate the true merits and genuine satisfaction of goodwill.

It is the contention of this author, after much soul searching, that goodwill towards all is better than money because, compared to money, goodwill will make you happier and the world a better place. Read on and we will show you why goodwill is better than money and how joining this Goodwill Revolution will make the world a better place.

So what is the goodwill revolution anyhow? The goodwill revolution is a down-with-money-up-with-people revolution. The Goodwill Revolution seeks to restore human values by emphasizing that humans are social beings by making a conscious effort to reach out to all people and to fight against the excesses of materialism, the materialism that has devalued humans and our values.

Allow me to introduce the product of the goodwill revolution, Goodwillism. Goodwillism is a philosophy which advocates that the prime guiding principle of life should be the creation of goodwill towards all regardless of race, religion, socioeconomic status, ethnicity, class, political party and so on. Ideas in Goodwillism may seem familiar. They are all not new, but in Goodwillism these ideas have been compiled, organized and marshalled in such a way as to impact our prevailing money-hogging rat race culture. And, not just to impact it, but to replace it with a better one. The ideas of Nelson Mandela and Dr. Martin Luther King play prominent roles. The spread of goodwillism requires revolution, hence the goodwill revolution.

Goodwillism is a realistic, practical movement to fight consumer mania, improve your life, the lives of others, your community and the world by promoting goodwill to all. "Goodwill to all" is not new. It is the original message of Christmas given to man by the angels. But, this message has languished on the back burner and plays little role in our present rat race-society. Now, through the Goodwill

Revolution, it will play a dominant role for the betterment of all.

You are invited to join the Goodwill Revolution and thus become a goodwillist or less formal name, a goodwillie. So, join the Goodwill Revolution against the addiction, worship and corrupting influence of money by organizing around 'goodwill to all' in order to achieve a more happy meaningful life, better relationships and build a better world. But, today Jamaica, tomorrow the world!

We have made astounding technological advances but our strife-filled world is falling apart like a great Humpty Dumpty. The villain is this corrupting influence of money on our values, political system, our leaders, justice, the media and our entire society in general. The Goodwill Revolution is a systematic comprehensive plan to put Humpty Dumpty back together again by harnessing the inherent goodness of man to fix the severe problems of society. It will seek to transform the plethora of adversarial relationships to amicable relationships. It will devalue money and revalue people.   It will unleash the unrecognized, unstoppable power of goodwill to overcome money mania to achieve real happiness.

Be Extra Nice to Everyone Every Time Regardless

Jamaicans will have to abandon and reject that mean-spirited rat race philosophy and adopt the goodwillism philosophy. The aim of the goodwillism philosophy is to make the world, not just Jamaica, a better place. Granted we have limited influence, but will not be deterred by that. Our music has captured the world. Goodwillism will make Jamaica a better place. The world will follow later.

We must seek to be extra nice to every one every time regardless. As a goodwillist, we must make a conscious effort to try to be, not just nice to everyone we encounter, but be the nicest we can be.

1. Befriend all – use goodwill to be a friend to everyone
2. Do good deeds
3. Appreciate and acknowledge good deeds - athletes, entertainers
4. Oppose bad and evil deeds but in such a way that goodwill is maintained with the perpetrator.
5. Proselytizing - Converting others and spreading the goodwillism philosophy

The Pillars of the Goodwill Revolution

1. Abandon Materialism –
   - Choosing to be happy rather than to be rich
   - Recognizing and resisting our addiction to money and materialism
   - Making a strong deliberate effort to reduce our appetite for material things.
   - Rejecting the manipulation, snobbery and propaganda of advertising
   - Making a conscious effort to be happy with less
   - Refusing to buy extravagant earth-resource-stripping products like gas guzzling SUV's, and hotel-size homes.
   - Admiring people on the basis of their good deeds and their character rather than on the amount of money they have or their celebrity status.

Actively seek goodwill to all with no exceptions

- Improve our relationships with family, friends and all people in general.
- Reach out to be a friend to all but especially those who differ from us by race, religion, nationality, ethnicity, politics, and so on.

- Make a special effort to get to know people better
- Try to find the good in all
- Try to overcome the fear of rejection in reaching out to befriend all
- Embrace goodwill to all including those who do not like us.
- Try to make sure that all interactions with people are positive and uplifting regardless of how obnoxious and belligerent the other person might seem to be.
- Constantly seek opportunities to do good deeds
- Acknowledge and appreciate the good deeds of others.

2. Oppose anything that destroys goodwill such as war, injustice, exploitation, derision
    - Oppose belligerence and hostility with goodwill.
    - Oppose bad and evil deeds but in such a way that goodwill is maintained with the perpetrator

3. Renounce aggressiveness, vengeance and belligerence; as anger distorts reason and good judgement
    - Choose reconciliation over retaliation and revenge
    - Shun retaliation and instead try to convert an enemy into a friend.

Goals

Goodwillists seek, to be less dependent on money, lots of friends, a warm friendly, fair and just environment, and a better world. To obtain lots of friends we need to improve our relationships with others. In our present society, relationships between people are too often just lukewarm.

This is because they have been trivialized and treated as unimportant. The main focus of the Goodwill Revolution is to use goodwill to improve and strengthen all sorts of relationships between people.

In simplest terms this goal is to become friends to everyone. We want to be friends with our spouses, our relatives, our neighbors, our co-workers, people we do not even know, people who do not even want to be friends with us, or as I said before everyone, the world.

Now I have heard many a motivational speaker, respected psychologists and similar professionals advise the opposite. These motivational speakers started off wrong anyhow. It seems that they always begin with some personal rags-to-riches story of their life that they are passing on and how they did it. So success to them is achieving these riches from rags. They have a lot of good advice but unfortunately they are reinforcing this money mania. Their message is not goodwill to **all** but to some, a **select few**. They want us to collect only the 'nice' people, the beautiful people, the positive people, the desirable people as friends. We are supposed to collect friends who enhance us. And, we should shun the other so-called negative people. I even heard one expert refer to these people unworthy of our friendship as 'toxic' people, people who will drag us down. Often, these are the people who really need friends. Of course, it is probably much easier and customary to put up these discriminating criteria and all sorts of qualifications on friends. Do you qualify to be their friend and do they qualify to be yours? I mention this to make it perfectly clear that these exclusions are completely opposite to goodwillism goals. When we say "*to all*" we mean "*to all*". Besides, our way should be different from the norm. It is after all a revolution, a goodwill-to-all revolution.

To improve relationships with people we have got to upgrade our relationship skills, our people skills. To do that we need to examine them closely and see how and where we can improve them. How do we treat people now and how can we do better?

Be a friend to everyone

"A stranger is a friend that I have not yet met." - Unknown

"I never met a man I did not like." – Will Rodgers

"I do not want any friends". My friend of many years said that to me with great conviction. I was lucky to be the exception but unfortunately such a statement is not uncommon among many people. It is a symptom of how our society has deteriorated until friends have become undesirable. Through the goodwill revolution we seek to reverse that. Our money centered culture has so devalued people that they are undesirable or unworthy of the effort as friends. We seek the comfort and refuge of money at the expense of friends. Besides, we fear our offer of friendship might expose us to the pain of rejection, the uncertainty of distrust, fear of insincerity and the risk of exploitation and vulnerability. Yes, so many withdraw to the security of money, of materialism and abandon fickle unreliable 'friends'.

So what is our society to become, a bunch of isolated money-seeking hermits? It seems headed that way but we goodwillists rebel against that trend. We do not go along with this devaluation of people. We revalue them. We consider people to be very important to our society. We, like the Quakers, seek a society of friends so we seek to befriend all. We unashamedly and without reservation seek goodwill towards all. This is the primary goal of the goodwill revolution. We want to befriend everyone.

We, goodwillists, are not afraid to admit that we want people to like us. We think this is a very worthy goal and a goal which most people share, but secretly.

Being a good friend makes you valuable. Here is the logic:

- A good friend is valuable.
- A good friend to some or all makes you valuable to some or all.
- A bad friend is not valuable.
- A bad friend is not valuable to anyone.

So be a good friend, even to a bad friend, and increase your worth.

This is not always easy, especially in our jaded society. In this quest to achieve it, we will face distrust, insincerity, exploitation and even ridicule. We have got to use all our skills, good judgment, all of our smarts, to overcome these real obstacles in order to accomplish this. Yes, we can anticipate strong opposition especially from the victims of the money addiction, but we must fight on.

The rhythm and blues group called War raised an important question in their lyrics. which asks instead, *"Why can't we be friends? Why can't we be friends?"*

I am a goodwillist means I *want to be friends with everyone.* It fully recognizes that this is a tall order if not virtually impossible to achieve. Besides people have all sorts of different criteria for friends. Regardless of what we do, we may never qualify. We can only control our actions. So, if we can't become friends with everyone, let us try to be friendly to everyone.

As goodwillists we must make a constant conscious effort to avoid the actions which discourage friendship and do those that make us more desirable. So we need to first of all investigate what are the traits that make us likable and the ones that make us unlikeable?

Like - Why do you like someone? Because they are:
1.funny
2. friendly
3. same race as you
4.pretty
5.smart and intelligent
6. kind
7.unselfish
8 good listener
9.interesting
10.pays attention to me
11 shows concern for me
12 shows concern for others
13 upbeat
14 laughs at my jokes
15 hates the same things I do
16 likes the same things I do
17 brave
18 educated
19 considerate
20 understanding
21 witty
22 fun-loving
23 serious
24 ambitious
25 honest
26 tactful
27 other ----------

Dislike - Why do you dislike someone? Because they are:
1.loud
2. Rude
3. Obnoxious
4. Stupid

5. Insulting
6. Inconsiderate
7. Selfish
8 uneducated
9. domineering
10 bossy
11 boring
12 too talkative
13 no sense of humor
14 mean
15 boastful
16 lecherous
17 unpopular, unliked by others
18 rich
19 other race or religion, nationality
20 derisive
21 belligerent
22 uncaring
23 constantly puts people down
24 profane
25 withdrawn
26 cowardly
27 insincere
28 lies
29 dishonest
30 steals
31 low status
32 poor/rich
33 unpopular with others
34 too complaining
35 snobbish
36 insensitive
37 ugly
38 fat/thin
39 bad dresser
40 ignores me
41 too depressing

42 too religious
43 too argumentative
44 too embarrassing
45 too unfriendly
46 too negative
47 too nosy
48 other -------------
Rank the top 10 in each category.

"*The unexamined life is not worth living*" or how do you stack up on your own rankings? Hopefully this self-examination will point out areas you need to improve.

As a goodwillist we must always strive to do things to make people feel good. Making someone the brunt of jokes is very popular but it does not make that person feel good. Derision, sarcasm, and ridicule do not make the subject of such actions feel good. It does the opposite.

Some examples:

- *Growing up as a kid in Jamaica, making fun of people was very popular. I remember racking my brains to come up with a great insult in order to gain respect among my friends. One of my creative bests was "you are a bombastic superflastic warra warra dead dog". That was a winner and I was very proud of it. When I called someone that, it got lots of laughs. How ridiculous! Of course, we are all familiar with probably the most popular method of humiliating someone is to curse them out with a barrage of our own unique profanity. Although this is considered vulgar and vile, Jamaicans use them often. So as a goodwillie, we must abandon 'bad wuds' and focus on words that will uplift spirits.*

- *I leave my home in Maryland to fly to Columbus, Ohio to watch and cheer on Jamaica in a qualifying World Cup football match. I arrive the day before the game. So that evening, I go to the hotel bar to*

> *meet up with other Jamaican supporters to rally round the team. There I find some loudmouth, not talking football, but launching some homophobic rant against some 'battyman'. I went back to my room.*

- *Another time I was on holiday in Negril. Again Jamaica was playing USA in a World Cup football qualifier. Jamaica had some crucial injuries and the US was highly favoured. Rather than stay in my Negril hotel, I sought out a local bar to join my fellow Jamaicans to cheer on our team. I was so enthusiastic about the occasion. Jamaica fell behind early and from that time, a couple of loudmouths dominated the bar, criticizing and berating the Jamaica coach and certain players. I wish I had stayed in my hotel.*

Recently I heard a Jamaican comedian on the web. This comedian' act was a steady stream of abusing the physical appearance of an American celebrity. It was in no way funny. As a Jamaican, I was embarrassed.

Too often in Jamaica we routinely put people down. The goodwill revolution routinely tries to lift people up.

So goodwillists must give up this type of unfriendly behavior. Too many have become so accustomed to using and accepting these traits as essential to making conversation interesting, that they might be reluctant to give them up. They feel compelled to display their acid wit by picking on someone for 'goodhearted' ribbing. It might seem trivial, but this 'goodhearted ribbing contributes to the acceptance of a certain meanness in our rat race culture. Remove some sort of derision from some people's conversation and they would be mute. As goodwillists we need to be on the lookout to avoid traits like these that make people feel bad. We might be very comfortable with them, even dependent on them, but they are not worth holding on to.

Enemy but no retaliation

Enemies are friends with problems.

What is an enemy? Someone we dislike? Not good enough. Someone who does bad things to us or to our friends?

It happens all the time . An enemy has done you a great wrong. He might have insulted your mother. He might have ridiculed you. He might have told an evil lie about you. He may have physically assaulted you. What do you do? Generally if someone does something mean to you then you want to retaliate by doing something even meaner to them. Retaliation means escalation. It's payback time. Even if a friend does something bad to you, you want to pay the friend back. But, let's take the worse case scenario. An enemy does something mean to you. Shouldn't we aim for the best most desirable outcome of that situation? The popular and acceptable response is to retaliate so severely that the enemy will not do it again.

But that is not **the best possible outcome**. The best possible outcome is that your enemy becomes your friend. And, if that is the best outcome, should we not do what it takes to achieve it? Goodwillists always go for the best possible outcome first.

So, instead of retaliation we seek reconciliation. But in order to reconcile, we have to forgive. With anger burning inside us, it can be tough to forgive. It is even better for your health to forgive.

We have to learn how to forgive. The anger, resentment and blame that many people hold on to, often for years can actually cause health problems. Learning how to forgive could prove to be curative. Negative emotions, such as anger, resentment and blame, can cause stress to build up in the body. Where there is excessive stress, there is the potential for all sorts of physical, mental and emotional problems. Most notably, elevated stress levels can impair the body's immune system, putting you at risk for heart disease, chronic pain and depression, among many other debilitating conditions. On the other hand, letting go of grudges and bitterness can make way for happiness, health and peace. This inability to forgive, "unforgiveness", can ruin our relationships, rob us of our happiness, and even impact our physical health.

Forgiveness can be heroic. Be a hero.
Twenty-one-year-old white racist Dylann Roof was welcomed into the Emmanuel AME church bible class in Charleston, South Carolina, USA. After one hour there, he took out a gun and systematically shot and killed nine black people, six women and three men. He reloaded the gun many times and several victims received multiple gun shots. He admitted shooting them because they were black. The survivors confronted him in court. They were in pain. They were crying. They were angry. But, they were heroic. I felt so proud of them. Despite all their pain. *"We forgive you". Yes, they offered their forgiveness to the cold-blooded killer!* The words of the daughter of one of the victims, Ethyl Lance, was typical of the group.
"I will never talk to her (her mother) ever again,,,,,,. "I will never be able to hold her ever again. But I forgive you." Or as a relative of the slain Rev. DePayne Middleton-Doctor said:
"I am a work in progress and I acknowledge that I am very angry. ....We are the family that love built. We have no room for hate so we have to forgive."

There are some other very practical reasons not to retaliate. Retaliation is pretty much not a rational but an emotional response. Emotions can make you do some pretty irrational things like retaliating and getting beaten to a pulp. Or retaliating and beating someone to a pulp and ending up in the hoosegow. *"I showed him, but it is so miserable here in jail!"* How often on the sports field, it is the one that retaliates that get penalized.

Do Good Deeds

I remember driving home in the US from work one evening. I was about two miles from home in heavy traffic, when suddenly my clutch seemed to have gone haywire. I struggled to maneuver the car to the shoulder, where it finally came to rest. Anger and frustration descended on me as I bemoaned my complete mechanical ignorance. Within seconds another car pulled over and out jumped a white youth.

"I saw you pull over. Problem?" he asked. I explained what happened and the next moment he was lying on the ground peering under my car.

"The clutch cable is broken. It's not too serious and the gas station across the way should be able to fix it." And he was gone without a "heigh-o silver!" "Who was that masked man?", I wondered. "To stop so spontaneously and help an old middle-aged black man that he did not know from Adam." The benevolence of the act overwhelmed my frustration and I felt good that sunmmer evening. Not only then, but when I think back about that kind spontaneous act, I feel good all over again.

A goodwillist strives to do good deeds. Good deeds make you feel good. It makes the person you did the good deed for feel good. Even people who observe the good deed feel good too. In fact doing a good deed can be more satisfying than buying a Lexus. The novelty of the fancy car soon wears off, the payments become onerous, and it does not generate the good feelings in others particularly.

A popular antidote for feeling unhappy, which does not really work, is to go out and, yes, buy something impulsively. Lots of people swear by that remedy, but let me emphasize. *"It does not work!"* I wonder who ever came up with that idea. Probably some Madison Avenue advertising exec. *"Just go into debt and you will feel better." "Buy something you do not need and you will feel better."* Get real. If you really want to feel better, do a good deed. Find someone to help. There is power in good deeds. They are therapeutic.

Savor good deeds

Good deeds make you feel good.. Savor them. If you do a good deed, make an effort to enjoy how it makes you feel good. If you see a good deed, enjoy it too and tell others about it so they can enjoy it too. In so doing we create a climate that will foster and stimulate goodwill.

Unfortunately they are those that will try to impose on your good deeds. You should not allow this as this might be exploitation. This is where again we must use good judgement, tact, and our communication skills. For although we should avoid this type of exploitation, at the same time we should do it in such a way as not to hurt the feelings of the potential exploiter.

Goodwill Quotient

We need to get in the habit of doing good deeds. We drive every day so be on the lookout to be courteous and yield the right of way to other drivers or pedestrians whenever we can. We spend most of our waking hours at work, so seek ways to be friendly and do good deeds to all your co-workers. The more we do them, the more conditioned we become and the easier it will be.

So doing good deeds are an essential part of being a goodwillist. When was the last time you did a good deed? I think tangible goals are a good thing so maybe goodwillists should set themselves a good deeds frequency target. How about at least one good deed per month? In order to establish some sort of our own personal measurement of our *goodwillistness*, we could use a sort of a goodwillist quotient (GQ). This good deeds frequency would then become a part of your GQ. So let us define GQ as the number of good deeds per year, which would mean that a frequency of 1 per month would be equivalent to a GQ of 12. Aim high!

Do it anyway
We have stated that doing good basically is its own reward. But, not always. Unfortunately, and much too often, we encounter ingratitude, *"sharper than the serpent's tooth"*. Yes, ingratitude, does hurt and can undermine your resolve to do good. Gratitude is nice, but don't expect it nor even set it as a condition. Do it anyway.

Fortunately a more comprehensive guide has already been established for goodwillists to follow. No description of goodwillism would be complete without it. It is the Paradoxical Commandments by Dr. Kent M. Keith.(originally quoted in my book, *"Boycott Money and Save Your Soul – Launcjing the Goodwill Revolution"*) Goodwillists, obey these commandments. Nail them up on a wall and check yourself from time to time.

The Paradoxical Commandments
by Dr. Kent M. Keith

1. People are illogical, unreasonable, and self-centered.
   Love them anyway.

2. If you do good, people will accuse you of selfish ulterior motives.
    Do good anyway.
3. If you are successful, you win false friends and true enemies.
    Succeed anyway.
4. The good you do today will be forgotten tomorrow.
    Do good anyway.
5. Honesty and frankness make you vulnerable.
    Be honest and frank anyway.
6. The biggest men and women with the biggest ideas can be shot down by the smallest men and women with the smallest minds.
    Think big anyway.
7. People favor underdogs but follow only top dogs.
    Fight for a few underdogs anyway.
8. What you spend years building may be destroyed overnight.
    Build anyway.
9. People really need help but may attack you if you do help them.
    Help people anyway.
10. Give the world the best you have and you'll get kicked in the teeth.
    Give the world the best you have anyway.

Goodwill can make you invincible

Extending goodwill to strangers is actually easy. But, maintaining goodwill to someone close to you, who has betrayed you, has stabbed you in the back, is really tough. Overcoming treachery is probably the biggest hurdle and is probably why so many relationships between family and friends have been poisoned. Enduring loss of trust and bitterness can come from the slightest of misdeeds too and especially among families. Feuding is just not allowed. Healing relationships is very important to goodwillists so be committed to using all your skills, patience and resolve to try to heal things. Good relationships are better than bad ones so why not work towards creating, maintaining and restoring good ones? It's hard. Your anger, your pride, your compulsion to retaliate, gets in the way. But, if you overcome these to maintain goodwill, a bonus lies ahead. The more you do this the stronger you will get and after awhile you will become invincible. Those knives in your back will bounce back and will no longer hurt you.

In addition, there are many who will try to abuse and exploit the very good deeds that you do. But, goodwillists do it anyway. But let me emphasize once again, goodwillists are required to use all their skills and wits and intelligence to use good judgment in the performance of these good deeds.

Triple 'A' them – Aware, Acknowledge, Appreciate

Ever been to a sports event? The batter hits a home run or the soccer player scores a goal. The spectators erupt in tremendous applause. They show their appreciation. Appreciation is so important. It is so important that it should not be given only to athletes and rock stars and just celebrities. Goodwillists should always strive to express their appreciation for good deeds. It is what the shrinks refer to as positive reinforcement. Good deeds make us feel good and by expressing appreciation we encourage the generation of more good deeds. Ok, so we don't have to jump up and cheer, but a simple compliment can do wonders. And, it is so easy to do.

Many people just love to criticize. Of course constructive, tactful, helpful criticism has an important role to play. But, alas, seldom that is the case. Overwhelmingly it is these destructive criticizers. Don't let these chronic criticizers suck you into their dogmatic world. Instead of constantly looking for bad things to criticize people, let's look for good things to compliment them. Too often good deeds go unnoticed or are taken for granted. Taking things for granted is the enemy of appreciation and is too commonplace. All good deeds are important and deserve to be noticed. We are probably so conditioned to ignoring good deeds but we must resist it. So before we can appreciate, we must be *A*ware of the good deed. To be aware we must pay attention. We must be vigilant for good deeds and must *A*cknowledge them. So, with regards to the performer of good deeds, goodwillists must resist taking them for granted and ***Triple A*** them instead. The triple A's are:

1.   Be **A**ware
2.   **A**cknowledge
3.   **A**ppreciate

Be **A**ware of good deeds, **A**cknowledge them, and show **A**ppreciation for them. In short, ***Triple A*** them.

Goodwillists should always be on the lookout for reasons and opportunities to compliment. Compliment good deeds, good service, good job, good performance...all the good things. I always go out of my way to compliment people as long as they deserve it. *Triple A them*. They don't have to perform Nobel-Peace-Prize-winning stuff too.

Certificate of Appreciation

A very important way to do good is to volunteer. Let us formally show our appreciation to volunteers. So, let us award to volunteers a written document to show appreciation. The certificate of appreciation would state , the name of the awardee, the date , task, number of hours involved and the name, signature and the contact information of the organizer of the volunteer service. The volunteer work should not be taken for granted or forgotten, so this Certificate of Appreciation would be a permanent reminder. Furthermore, it would become a part of the volunteer's resume in job seeking and serve as a reference.

Everyday Goodwillist

We have got to incorporate goodwillist traits in our everyday life so that it becomes a habit. We drive every day. Don't let other drivers cut you off. Beat them to the punch and yield the right of way to them. We go to a restaurant or the supermarket and encounter a surly server or clerk. Most people react by trying to out-surl them. Others avoid such persons, but, as a goodwillist, I seek out the surly person and try to make them cheerful. I do it all the time and my unexpected friendly reaction usually shocks the surliness out of them. I feel good and they feel good. Mission accomplished.

Most of your waking hours are spent at work. So the workplace is a good place to hone and practice your goodwillist skills. Be sure to befriend all co-workers but go even beyond that. Consider your co-workers and you a team and try to generate team spirit. Having played sports all my life, I think the camaraderie it engendered was even better than the sport itself. So, why not in the ordinarily dreary workplace too?

Unique

It would be unrealistic and even unfair for many of those who spent their lives acquiring material things to throw them away in order to join the Goodwill Revolution. Such a transition is probably very tough. We want to bring people together, even those that reject the Goodwill Revolution. But I think it is reasonable to no longer make materialism to continue to be their life's goal. Stop that and welcome to the Goodwill Revolution

But, this goodwill revolution is unique from other revolutions. Many other revolutions, despite their outstanding merits, have had their reign of terror. But not the goodwill revolution. For goodwill is our goal and also our means to achieve that goal. We will win over our opponents with goodwill. We will seek to make friends of them, to convert them to be goodwillists too.

But, don't expect gratitude, appreciation or even positive results right away. Many people are so (conditioned) screwed up by the rat race, that they will be cynical and suspicious. Some will even try to exploit our goodness. Give them time. Persevere.

The more converts we make, the better our environment becomes. We are making a better Jamaica at least one person at a time. But, don't be impatient.

Chapter 10

Poor but Proud – Inferior no more

If you are a genuine goodwillie you are second to none even if you are poor.

In Jamaica and all over the world, our money-hogging rat-race society, poor people must suffer a severe inferiority complex. Being poor, they have inferior home (if they have homes at all).They have inferior education. They have inferior policing. In Jamaica, they dare not enter through the front door. They generally do not have an automobile and must rely on public transportation. They have unskilled poor paying jobs. They have lousy healthcare. They are looked down upon by the rest of society. Granted a few make it out of poverty but the chances of getting out of this hole are pretty slim. Education and entrepreneurship are touted as the way up, but in reality, the vast majority is stuck in poverty and to be poor its's an awful stigma for life. It is this money-hogging rat race culture of materialism that relegates the poor to feelings of inferiority and the rich to superiority. And when you throw in Jamaica's rigid class system, it is even worse.

What is so special about an expensive fancy car? It is ostentatious and showy. If every Jamaican had one, there would be no room on the roads to accommodate them. The roads would be so crowded that they would become parking lots. They are actually bad for Jamaican economy as they are so expensive that they drain away Jamaica's limited foreign currency. They burn more gas, so increase Jamaica's dependence on oil.

Do you remember that old Jamaican rhyme from way back when the devil was a boy?:

"The white gal ride in motor car
The brown gal do the same
The black gal ride in donkey cart

But she riding just the same.:

So take those more efficient minibus for "we riding just the same".
Of course these expensive automobiles grant status to their owners and so many onlookers salivate to own one. I think their greatest attraction is that they impress others.
 But, not me. As country singer Shania Twain sings, "they don't impress much." Also, the big palatial houses 'don't impress me much". Once I saw a big fancy yacht with a helicopter and heliport on it. But guess what? It "did not impress me much". Owners of these baubles revel in the attention and admiration that they receive. But for goodwillists these are just *sounding brass and tinkling cymbals, signifying nothing.*
That does not impress goodwillists much. Your money and your wealth does not impress us. Regardless if you are rich or poor, you impress us if you are kind, compassionate, stand up for justice, helpful, generous, etcetera. In the materialistic rat race these qualities are liabilities, while greed and selfishness are assets.
It is said that the new golden rule is, "*He who has the gold make the rules.*" That is indeed the golden rule for the materialistic rat race culture.   But, for the goodwill revolution we follow the original golden rule. "*Do unto others as you would have them do unto you*".
Compulsive irrational buying mania
 – "*A shine eye gal is a trouble to a man*".
Do you remember that old Jamaican song about a "shine-eye gal".

A shine eye gal iis a trouble to a man
A shine eye gal iis a trouble to a man
For she wants and she wants everything
For she wants and she wants everything

A shine-eye gal is a pretty girl, but the song warns that "A shine-eye gal is a trouble to a man for she wants and she wants and she wants everything". We have become conditioned with a compulsive irrational buying mania like the "shine-eye gal" to want and to want and to want everything.

Moral Superiority

Goodwillies aim to be better than everyone else. This is not an arrogant statement. This is because to be better than anyone else, one has to be morally superior. In our competitive society, we goodwillies compete to be morally superior because that competitiveness will produce a better Jamaica. For to be morally superior you have to be kinder, fairer, more just, more compassionate, more honest, and so on. Morally superior persons don't kill, don't pollute the atmosphere to make an extra buck, don't exploit and victimize workers, don't drop 2-ton bombs in a residential neighborhood in Iraq, and so on.

In our society today, money and power rule and dominate. But this is a revolution, a goodwill revolution. Money and power will define esteem no more. The better person is the morally superior person. And it is really democratic. Money and power are irrelevant. It does not matter if you are rich or poor, black or white, Christian or Muslim, or all those other categories people find themselves, you have equal opportunity to be morally superior. So I don't care how much money you have Bill Gates, you are not better than I. Your obnoxious, repressive, unfair, unjust boss at work is a nobody for all his power over you. Why? Because he is obviously very morally inferior. In reality he is a pitiful figure running amok. So thank God you are not cursed with his obvious character flaws. *There but for the grace of God go I*".

So with such a perspective, moral superiority can give you the power to endure. It is fortifying. I think it is what Shakespeare meant when Brutus said in Julius Caesar, *"There is no terror, Cassius, in your threats, for I am so well armed in honesty, that they pass me by, like the idle wind , that I respect not."*
So rich people, especially those who exploited others to gain their wealth, and the repressive boss are all *"like the idle wind which I respect not"*. I wish I could help them.
Of course rich people will still look down on the poor, but as long as any poor person is morally superior, then such rich persons are deluded and should be ignored. Who cares what they think? Be good and be proud.

Chapter 11

Tourism – the Good, the Bad and the Ugly

Tourism is the single most important generator of foreign exchange for the Jamaican economy, It employs the second largest number of Jamaicans (approx. 200,000) both directly (in hotels, transport, attractions, and craft), as well as indirectly (trading, manufacturing, banking, etc. mainly in and around resort towns).
However, I have witnessed some adverse side effects of tourism which the Goodwill Revolution can fix.

- I took the airport shuttle from Montego Bay to Negril. All the other passengers were white. They received excellent treatment at their hotel destinations. The driver was very professional, driving them right up to their luxury hotel, removing and lugging their luggage inside, displaying a great positive attitude. But, when he came to my hotel, he parked outside on the road and pointed up the driveway to my hotel. I did not move until he reluctantly drove up the driveway and then parked. Money rears its ugly head again. Obviously, white tourists have more money and tip better than black tourists. So, the white tourists in general probably get better service than black tourists. I have had a similar experience trying to hail a taxicab in Washington D.C. Money has the power to make black Jamaicans discriminate against their fellow black people! The goodwill revolution solution is for these workers to give excellent service to all tourists regardless of their perceived race or economic status.

- I have also noticed that the craft vendors are not particularly friendly to each other. Once again money is the root cause. I don't see how these vendors can make a living in this occupation. Their fellow vendors are competitors for little money. They are forced to jockey with each other to get that scarce tourist buck. So they become nice to tourists but hostile to each other. They see tourists as a meal ticket but see colleagues as competitors for that meal ticket

- I spoke with a hotel waitress. She gets a poor salary and is just a contract employee. Contract employee means she works for a limited time, no permanent employment, no vacation, no sick leave and no promotion. However, she is grateful to have a job.

- Right there on the beach, I saw a hotel security guard trying to prevent a vendor from harassing a guest to buy his wares. The security guard was an old man. The vendor finally obeyed the guard but not before menacing and hurling a torrent of abusive profanity at him. Fortunately it did not escalate into violence.

- One morning I felt for some nice ackee and saltfish for breakfast. Besides, I like to patronize the small local entrepreneurs. So, I asked a local Jamaican on the beach for directions to such a restaurant. He suggested I follow him to the restaurant but that I buy him breakfast too. I refused because I did not want to encourage locals to charge money just to be helpful and polite.

I am sure that all over tourist regions in Jamaica, good people are being corrupted in this way. What a shame! But, the goodwill revolution can fix this so that everyone benefits and mutual respect and 'goodwill' prevails.

Chapter 12

Reducing Crime

Jamaica Exile
by Michael Irving Phillips

Imprisoned in my home sweet home
Behind iron bars
That lets in the sunshine
But keeps out crime
Is not for me,
Anymore

For Jamaica bleeds
Stabbed in the heart repeatedly
By ruthless thugs of crime
And Jamaicans die
And fear death
Even behind their iron bars
That let in sunshine
But keeps out crime

And because of these
Ruthless thugs of crime
Jamaicans leave
Exiled to a foreign land
To leave behind
Distrusted politicians
Trapped in stereotypes
To serve a cynical public
And hopelessly watch
As crime plan after new crime plan
Fails
And even innocent children die
And heartless thugs triumph

To leave behind their

Yam and sweet potato
For foreign fast cholesterol-filled food
Leave behind their tropic nights
Filled with reggae music
Leave behind their seas so blue
Before it runs red
With the blood of Jamaica
Before laughter turns to screams
Before laughter turns to slaughter

To leave all that behind
For exile
In some uncaring foreign land
For anonymity
To adopt a foreign culture
And live in the memory
Of a crime-free Jamaica
Without iron bars
To let in sunshine
And to keep out crime
It is not a life
Without Jamaica
I am alive
But I am not kicking

The greed and the ruthlessness of the dehumanizing money-chasing rat race culture serve as a catalyst for crime. The greatest challenge to improving the quality of life in Jamaica is the removal of the menace of crime. Police protection has failed to provide an acceptable level of safety as homicide and violent crimes continue at high rates. Remedial plans run from enlightened to draconian but crime continues to soar. New police chiefs come and go. There is an abundance of finger-pointing, but like the babbling brook, crime goes on forever. So how will the goodwill revolution succeed where so many other proposals have failed dismally?

What type of crimes terrorize Jamaica? They are not embezzling millions. They are not committing insider trading. They do lock up a lot of people for the victimless crime of doing drugs. But it is the crimes that victimize others which can make Jamaica a living hell. Let's spell it out. It is crimes such as theft, assault, murder, rape, mugging that we have to eliminate to transform our country into a magnificent community.

The goodwilliist way

People do not want to hurt people. It is unnatural. Jamaicans do not want to hurt Jamaicans. It is unnatural. The solution lies in appealing to the innate goodness in man. Punishment is not enough. We need to ask them to stop. We need to make them realize the folly of their actions. We need to convince criminals that they are better off without a life of crime. We need to convince them that instead of victimizing people they should be helping people. We need to find them, identify them and convince them to join the goodwill revolution. We need to dialogue with them.

The Stupidity of Crime

Firstly, we must take a look at some of the main reasons why people in Jamaica commit crimes.

- Money
- Domestic violence
- Desperation
- Vengeance
- Respect and recognition

Once again that root of all evil, money – the love of money, rears its ugly head. And most of these crimes are not for much money, just petty crimes. Criminals have killed for a

lousy pair of tennis shoes, an old broken-down bicycle, ridiculous things. Most of these crimes are committed in poor communities. Horrible crimes, ranging from brutal murder down, are often committed for very little money.
It is very little money because in the poor communities, no one has much money. Criminals are risking death, incarceration, injury, life as a fugitive for chicken feed. But worst of all, they end up being hated and despised by the overwhelming majority in their own communities as well as the rest of Jamaica.

Risks of crime
- Death
- Incarceration
- Injury
- Hate and despised by others
- Fugitive life

Crime as a job offers **no** sick leave, **no** paid holidays, **no** paid vacation, **no** health insurance and **no** pension,
- Crime is a very stupid choice
- Crime is low-paying in most cases generally
- Crime is loathsome and despicable
- Crime is dangerous
- Crime is evil
- Crime is disgusting –

Effects of crime on the arrested
Being arrested can affect:
- Your income
  If you are in jail, you will be unable to continue to work to pay bills. If you have a family how much more devastating that would be.
- Relationships with loved ones
  If you are incarcerated for months, years, or lifetime. Your spouse or significant other will be having sex

with someone else and you will not, at least not with consenting adults. A study done at the University of Illinois says difficulties in adjusting to separation and loss have led to depression and other mental health problems among prisoners and their families.

- Future employment opportunities
Many employers conduct criminal background checks before hiring new workers, so your ability to get a job later in life can be affected.

- Quality of life
With your freedom denied, how awful to live day after day after month after month after year after year in a 6x8 foot cell with your main furniture a toilet. Never to have a beer with the guys or grabbing a pattie from Spicy Patties.

Crime sure sounds like an awful job! Who would take such a job? Unfortunately, for some, this seems to be the only choice. But, for most, they get sucked into such a rotten occupation with their eyes closed, driven by desperation and not realizing just how disastrous a choice they have made. As goodwillists we need to steer the youth from that career path. Any job is better than that.

The growing menace of gangs

Poor youths are the worst victims with regards to employment. Their unemployment rate is very high. So, they have no jobs, no skills, no worthwhile education, and consequently no hope. So what if they made some bad decisions as kids? They do not deserve a life sentence for that. No jobs, no money no respect, no hope. Without these you are nobody. Where can they turn to? The rat race society is harshest on people like that. It makes them feel

unwanted. Who wants them? Who will take them in? I know. Gangs. Join a gang. Belong to a gang. Gangs will take them in. So, with the pressure of the rat race, gangs become very attractive to these rejected social outcasts.
Gangs offer them:
- Sense of Belonging
- Identity
- Protection

There have been all sorts of draconian measures to curtail gangs but gangs continue to proliferate. The appeal of gangs to rejected youth is virtually unstoppable. Instead we have to reach out and have these gang members join a better gang, a gang that will make them feel like they belong, restore their self-dignity, offer them protection and identity. This better gang is their community..
Community Actions – appeal to their innate goodness to help create an all-inclusive community. Instead of keeping them out, invite them in and enlist their help.
- Establish a liaison person to communicate with gangs
- Invite them to join a bigger gang – the community
- Urge them to be a gang for good – a goodwillist gang
- Point out "the stupidity of crime"
- Get their self-respect and respect of the community back

Transforming gangs
In Jamaica, we have to persuade gang members to make the intelligent choice. To become any type of leader, one has to be intelligent. A leader is responsible to his followers. A gang leader is responsible to his members, We have already established that crime is stupid so as a leader he should steer them away from a 'stupid' life of crime. .So, instead of rejection and disdain, he should find some way to

make them join our gang, the community. It is a very difficult solution, but it is the only solution.

Yes, it is time for gang members to wise up and join the Goodwill Revolution. Gang violence is the rat race on steroids. Spread goodwill to all instead of fear, terror, and murder. If you cannot find a job then join the volunteers in your community. It would make a wonderful impression if a gang would do something as simple as clean up litter in their community just one day per month. So, instead of hanging around and risk getting into trouble, they should do something productive, something that will earn the respect and admiration of their community.

Gang leaders can use their leadership skills to benefit the community by becoming community leaders.

But it is not all up to them. Goodwillist police and community leaders must be willing and ready to welcome these prodigal sons back. All sides must be prepared to replace hostility, animosity and belligerence with goodwill, cooperation and mutual respect.

Chapter 13

Babylon No More

The cradle of crime

About 10 years ago, I was on vacation in Ocho Rios. On the beach I met a Rasta, who was selling fruits out of some ragged make-shift barely-seaworthy but brightly-decorated floating contraption. (Did not qualify as a boat.) He was typical of so many there who work hard against great odds to make an honest living. During conversation he told me that the night before he had been robbed of the money he made. He even knew who the robber was. "*Did you report it to the police?*" I asked. It turned out that was a ridiculous question. Would the police investigate or even listen to his complaint?" *No way,*" he said. They were likely to tell him " *Gooway and nuh bother us*" if not abusing him too.

Can you imagine how helpless and frustrated this victim must feel? To be sure this crime is no one time occurrence. The victim can look forward to this happening over and over and over again after regular intervals. On the other hand, the robber probably has a whole network of victims. And, I am sure this type of thing goes on in many other poor neighborhoods all over Jamaica.

Of course some victims might not take it lying down. They might get a gun and seek redress. Or they might get a group of friends to beat their money out of the robber. But, the robber has buddies too and soon full-fledged gang warfare is underway.

Not only can this lead to gang warfare, assault and battery and even murder, but if the perpetrator is unchecked by police and gets away with his crime over and over again, it will embolden him. So he will step up from crimes against the poor to small business and on to the middle class. Make sure your burglar bars are intact.

The reality is that poor people are the greatest victims of crime and the police do not or are perceived as not protecting them, except for murder or other sensational crimes. It is dismissed as just petty crime. But it is not petty to some poor person barely eking out a living.

So, why should poor people cooperate with police if the police do not protect them, do not care about them, and are more likely to hassle them. And poor people constitute an overwhelming majority of our citizens, so a better relationship with the police is essential to the society.

I should point out that Jamaica is by no means unique in this, but this type of thing is typical in the US and probably all over the world.

The fact of the matter is that poor people are entitled to equal protection by police and they do not get it. The consequences are dire. Robbing and victimizing the poor becomes the training ground for criminals. So, if we are serious about fighting crime, we need to give extra protection to the poor and make that a top priority. Stop these beginners before they become hardened professional criminals.

Blessed are the peacemakers, Community Peacemakers

Prevention of crime is better than curing it. One of the better ways of preventing crimes is by community peacekeepers. These would intervene to resolve minor disputes such as family matters, petty theft, fights before they explode. They would be trained in conflict resolution and have a friendly personality, In order to obtain the trust of participants, they must maintain confidentiality especially from police.

As discussed before, many poor people are afraid to go to the police. with minor complaints. Instead, they could go to the community peacekeepers for help. The previous account of the rasta who was robbed repeatedly of his income made from selling nick-nacks from his "boat" by the same person. He could appeal to the community peacekeeper for help. If he is afraid to do even that, then a witness or anyone who is aware of that could enlist the help of the community peacekeeper.

The peacemaker would then mediate with the robber, pointing out :

- the "stupidity" of his crime considering the potential consequencies for such little money
- the misery it causes on his victim
- the need for people to live together in peace and harmony

In another scenario a 7-year-old kid steals the toy of another 7-year old. Even at that level, intervention is needed. In this instance, the community peacemaker would say something like this to the thief:

- :Do you know you could go to prison for stealing?
- Do you know that in prison you would not be able to see you dear parentsr only by visits?
- Do you know how much your dear parents would miss you? They would cry.
- Do you want to make your parents cry?.
- Do you know you would not be able to play with your friends again?
- Do you know you would not be able to go to the movies or to a football game?
- The victim probably hates you for robbing him.
- Do you want people to hate you?
- There is too much hate in the world so lets try to be friends with the victim instead."

This peacemaker could be heading off a kid from a life of crime. It is a valuable job. This person could be a volunteer, but deserves to be paid.

Educate them

Several slip into crime because of ignorance.

Informers have a bad name. But we have to make a choice. Do we inform and help the victim? Or, do we remain silent and help the criminal?

Fisticuffs might break out. Often the combatants are egged-on. And, the winner might even be congratulated. Everyone likes a winner. He is often congratulated for winning but he might not have been in the right. He might have been just a bully. He might have committed a simple assault on an innocent victim. Under these circumstances such congratulations might be supporting "might is right". So at times, the victim, hurting from a black-eye and a bleeding swollen lip, must also deal with the humiliation of losing the fight. This philosophy occurs too often in the world today and even on a country-to-country level. We need to always stand up for the right.

Besides, instead of encouraging fighters, we should be peacemakers. Sometimes even simple disputes explode into vicious outcomes, even murder. I read recently that a member of Jamaica's women's national soccer team was stabbed to death ina dispute over a cell phone. Regrets don't mean much after a person is killed. If the police were at the dispute. there would have been no murder, no prison term. If a peacemaker was at the dispute, there would have been no murder, no prison time. I wonder if anyone egged them on.

For A Lousy Cell Phone
by Michael Irving Phillips

For a lousy cell phone
The victim will no longer
Dribble the field
Of the National Stadium
To the cheers of hundreds
Ringing in her ears
The worms will eat her coffined body
In silence

For a lousy cellphone
The killer sunk her knife
For a lousy cellphone
The killer took her life
Regrets will not bring her back
For a lousy cell phone
You have given up your freedom
For living in a cell
For the rest of your life.
For a lousy cellphone
You will never own a cellphone
You will never touch a cellphone
For the rest of your life

For a lousy cellphone
You took a life
And threw away yours
What have you gained?
Nothing,
But the hatred of Jamaica
The cellphone may be smart
But you are stupid.
Very stupid

Education is the key. Every Jamaican should be educated in
conflict resolution. We need to include in the curriculum of

schools a civics course which would include conflict resolution, goodwillism, the stupidity of crime and even sex education. Conflict resolution is the process by which two or more parties reach a peaceful resolution to a dispute. A conflict resolution course is being taught already in some schools in Jamaica, but it should be required in all schools. Instead of just the three R's, schools should also prepare students to cope with the complexities and responsibilities of adulthood and to be better citizens.

We should not be ignoring very minor crimes, as unchecked, they are likely to grow into major crimes. For such small crimes we could treat them like we do the penalty for traffic infractions in some countries. There, they issue warnings and tickets and follow up with sending perpetrators to traffic school. I say for those who commit small offences we should include crime school in their punishment.

Missing ingredient
The latest crime reduction plan the Government has come up declaring State of Emergencies and designating Zones of Special Operations (ZOSA) to fight crime in selected high crime areas.. ZOSA is basically a state of emergency but covers a smaller area. States of emergency typically trample some human rights. Even if these reduce crime, it is not feasible to have a state of emergency indefinitely in these zones. The objectives sounded very reasonable:

- to provides a respite in the number of murders,
- to expand the number of law enforcement personnel on the ground,
- to restrict the free movement of criminals
- to gives regular policing an increased ability to work.

It seemed to be working and the public seemed pleased. Initial results were good, but despite these states of emergencies, official figures from the Jamaica Constabulary

Force (JCF) show that the number of murders committed in Jamaica up to October 12, 2019 for the same period the previous year have actually gone up from 997 to 1,026.

Crime plans come and go and often achieve limited success but usually are not sustainable. But, there is a missing ingredient. For any crime reduction plan to work, it must have strong public support, trust and cooperation. In recent times, instead of cooperation there has been confrontation. Trust has to be re-established between the police and members of the public, particularly the poor. So asking for this support is not enough. The missing ingredient, therefore, is a focus and concerted effort to build a better relationship between communities and police. Years ago my newsletter, Hot Calaloo, proposed a good way to do this by DWP, Dialogue With People.

DWP, Dialogue With People

DWP is essentially holding town meetings between the public and public officials in neighborhoods which are obvious hot spots of crime. It is evident that citizens perceive that they do not have an opportunity to make their concerns and frustrations heard, so they take to the streets to do just that.

These town hall meetings can be a valuable safety valve and at the same time allow valuable face-to-face exchange of information. I think the police can learn a lot from this and at the same time can convey the human side of the magnitude and danger of the job they have to do. People need to know how difficult the job of a policeman is. Too often they receive undeserved criticism and not the appreciation they deserve when they do a good job. Goodwillism in these instances require that we *Triple A* them, be **A**-ware of their good performance, **A**-cknowledge it and show **A**-ppreciation. The DWP meeting would be a great place to exhibit this.

DWP Meeting

This is a very important event so should be planned down to the smallest detail for maximum effectiveness.

Features of the meeting would include:

- Meetings would be held indoors in an area schoolhouse, church hall or similar venue large enough to hold a big crowd.
- Area residents should be invited and encouraged to attend to state their complaints, participate, and to listen and learn for themselves.
- Rules of order should be made known ahead of time, and adhered to.
- These rules should include time limits on complaints and decorum.
- Free refreshments should be considered as free food has a mellowing effect which might be very valuable.
- Very tight security for obvious reasons
- Meeting should be recorded on videotape to review and address matters arising from the meeting; to evaluate achievement, to make future improvement for subsequent meetings, for PR reasons: which might include TV broadcast
- Follow-up meeting or regularly scheduled meetings.

Attendees

Attendees would include, moderator, special guests and the public consisting of area residents.

A skilled moderator should ensure real dialogue. This is the most critical person to the success of this event. The most important aspect is dialogue. Those typical private investigations with multi-page report do not reach the man-in-the-street. Someone standing at a podium lecturing with a few token questions answered will not qualify as real dialogue.

Special Guests

There will be essentially two types of special guests. The first will be high officials, Government and otherwise, who will serve to add prestige and show support for the undertaking. The second type will be high officials to serve as authoritative sources, to address complaints, be accountable, and share information. These special guests should be carefully chosen and should include:

- Police representation ideally the Commissioner, Minister of Security, and local policeman skilled in PR
- Political party reps but they must agree beforehand on the mission of harmony and understanding and not pushing their own agenda
- Area religious and other community leaders

Expected benefits

Citizens and police will obtain a better understanding of each other.

- Citizens will be able to vent their anger and frustration in a productive manner without violence and civic disruptions
- Police will really get the perspective of the poor citizens
- Certain myths and misconceptions will be cleared up.
- Previously unknown community leaders will emerge and can be utilized as a resource to build harmony and cooperation.
- Special community committees may be formed such as, a Neighborhood Watch committee, a joint police-citizens review board to monitor police actions in the community, a refreshment committee to provide refreshment for DWP meetings, and most important, a police-citizen liaison committee to improve police-citizen relations and so on.

Police-Citizen Community Liaison Committee

The police-citizen liaison community committee is of special importance. As its name implies, it would be composed of police and community leaders. Victims of crime who are afraid to go to the police could seek out the committee or individual members to get justice done.

Let's do it!

Let's do it! Let's reason together. To be sure there are risks. The meeting could deteriorate into a big hostile public squabble. But the potential rewards are great. For the citizens, it could gain them the understanding, respect, protection and real commitment from the police.

The police have even more to gain. Right now the police are called Babylon, reflecting the distrust and suspicion many Jamaicans have for them. They could be *"Babylon"* no more. They could gain an appreciation of the peril, complexity and difficulty of their job. Instead of enmity, suspicion and contempt, they stand to gain appreciation, support and cooperation. This is bound to boost morale on the force, increase job satisfaction and make them more effective in fighting the real criminals that now terrorize our beloved island.

Chapter 14

Fill Your Pockets or Fill Your Soul

The primary goal
Shall we fill our pockets or shall we fill our soul? Do you want to be happy or rich? Which is your primary goal? Goodwillies want to be happy. Everyone thinks they want to be happy but what they really want to be is to be rich. So the few that actually become rich, lots of money, find out that , surprise!, that they are not happy. Many of us assume that if we become rich, happiness will be automatic. All our dreams will come true. Lots of rich people are unhappy. Now if you are rich and unhappy, what is the value of your wealth?

Feasibility
Which is a more feasible goal for the Jamaican population, to be rich or to be happy? There is no question in my mind that it is much easier to be happy than rich. Only a minority of people can be rich. Can we be happy without being rich? Sure we can. So if we are happy, why do we need to be rich. Some people will say they want to be rich and happy. But once again if you are happy, why do you need to be rich? The fact of the matter is to be happy and to be rich are two distinct goals. Each goal requires different actions.
I know many people are conditioned to think money is better than happiness. Would you give up riches to be happy? I know many who have. Yes, they gave up the fancy car, the palatial residence, substantial income and even luxurious lifestyle just to be happy. The gave that all up because of a process called divorce.

According to the Bible
If we turn to the Bible scriptures, there you will find the strongest support for goodwillie principles. These days the

true message of Christmas is lost in a buying frenzy. The true message is "Peace on earth. Goodwill towards all men." Christmas should be a big peace festival, a special time to promote goodwill towards all men instead of the awful commercialisation it now represents. This is not just a Christmas message, but it is the inspiration for goodwillies and the Goodwill Revolution. If we want peace on earth, we have to have goodwill towards all men. Just as the Christmas message has been distorted to buy, buy, buy to excess, so also has our lives been distorted to buy, buy, buy to excess. And as religious as we claim to be our true god becomes "money", money to buy, buy, buy to excess.

Despite what your preacher says, the Bible is clear and consistent on this point. "You cannot serve God and mammon." (Luke Chapter 16 v 13) Mammon is money, wealth, riches. When a rich man came to Jesus Christ and asked what should he do to achieve eternal life. We goodwillies are not as extremist as Christ, when he told the rich man to sell all that he had, give the proceeds to the poor and follow Him. When he refused, Christ said "It is easier for a camel to pass through the eye of a needle, than for a rich man to enter into the kingdom of God." (Luke Chapter 18 v 25)

Christ threw the money lenders out of the temple. But, guess what? They're back. The church and big money are intertwined. Fundamentalist churches like the Moral Majority in America are economic empires themselves.

The bible is relentless in attacking the pursuit of money as a goal. However, this message is strangely absent from our contemporary rich religious leaders. We goodwillies clearly have the bible on our side on this issue.

In the Bible, Paul raises the question of what is the greatest virtue? He then went on to reduce it to three finalists. In justifying his selection of his top choice, Paul produced some of the most quoted and most beautiful verses in the Bible. When I was younger, the translation identified them

as faith, hope and charity. The contemporary translation now has changed charity to love. There is a big difference between charity and love. Charity denotes a sense of giving, a sharing of ones fortunes with the less fortunate. The dictionary defines it as *"an act of feeling of benevolence, goodwill or affection"*.
Love is even harder to define. There are all sorts of love, romantic love, puppy love, maternal love, kinky love. Love uplifts, hurts, ennobles. As a popular Jamaican song asks *"If love's so good, how come it feels so bad?"* Everyone seems to have a different understanding of what love is and is the basis of many types of action, some good, some bad. Love is different things to different people. Oscar Wilde said:

"Yet each man kill the thing they love
By each let this be heard
Some do it with a bitter look
Some with a flattering word
The coward does it with a kiss
The brave man with a sword."

For these reasons I think the translators could have come up with a more appropriate word. The meaning of goodwill is unmistakable so I think this is much more appropriate. So here the revision of the Corinthians selected verses from Chapter 13: (King James version)

"1 Though I speak with the tongues of men and of angels; and have not goodwill, I am become as sounding brass and tinkling cymbal.
2 And though I have the gift of prophecy, and understand all mysteries, and all knowledge; and though I have all

faith, so that I could remove mountains; and have not goodwill, I am nothing.
3 And though I bestow all my gifts to the poor, and though I give my body to be burned, it profiteth me nothing.
....
11 When I was a child, I spake as a child, I thought as a child: but when I become a man, I put away childish things.
12 For now we see through a glass, darkly; but then face to face I know in part; but then I shall know even as I am known.
13 And now abideth faith, hope and goodwill, these three, but the greatest of these is goodwill."

Pope Francis chose to fill his soul

Pope Francis is the 266th and current Pope of the Catholic Church. He has rejected the materialistic privileges of his office such as:

Instead of a fancy chauffeured limousine he drives around in a humble Fiat.

Instead of living in the regal Vatican residence, he chose a simple Vatican guesthouse.

Instead of the glitzy gold, rich velvet, regal fur he chose to wear mainly a simple white cassock and sensible black shoes.

Even while he was a cardinal, he carried his own bags when travelling, , preferred public transportation to chauffeur-driven limousines, and, in one of his first acts as pope, he stopped by the hotel where he stayed before the conclave that elected him pope to settle his bill himself.

Uruguay President chose to fill his soul

President José "Pepe" Mujica of Uruguay , a 78-year-old former Marxist guerrilla who spent 14 years in prison, mostly in solitary confinement, rejected materialism for the simple life. He was the 40th President of Uruguay between 2010 and 2015. For example:

- He rejected the materialistic perks of the presidency.
- He refused to live at the Presidential Palace choosing instead to live in a one-bedroom house on his wife's farm.
- He refused to have a motorcade.
- Instead of a fancy chauffeured limousine in 2015 he was driving a 1987 Volkswagen Beetle.
- He donates over 90% of his $12,000/month salary to charity so he makes the same as the average citizen in Uruguay .

When called *"the poorest president in the world,"* Mujica says he is not poor. *"A poor person is not someone who has little but one who needs infinitely more, and more and more. I don't live in poverty, I live in simplicity. There's very little that I need to live."*

I hope Jamaican political leaders take a page out of his book.

Fill Your Soul

The problem is that all over the world we have been filling our pockets. The result - Lebanon, Chile, Iraq, Haiti, England, America, Ecuador, Algeria, Honduras, Colombia, Bolivia, Hong Kong, Libya, Spain are all erupting with despair and discontent (*October 2019*). Which country will be next? These are desperate times. These desperate times require the Goodwill Revolution. Let us fill our souls. Let us not fight fire with fire. Let us instead fight fire with the Goodwill Revolution. We don't want the Goodwill Revolution to lie dormant in some obscure book

In fact, this book is not just a book, but it is an invitation to join the Goodwill Revolution. Proclaim it to your friends, relatives and to as many as you can. Be a pioneer. Jamaican politicians, JLP and PNP, churches, all organisations that care about Jamaica and the people in general, should embrace and promote the Goodwill Revolution

Let us all spread the word. Let us use radio, fliers, internet, celebrities, word-of-mouth, door-to-door, church pulpits, sporting events, special concerts etc.. The more the merrier. In Jamaica, goodwillism should become our national policy. Right now, Jamaica and other countries have no stated national policy, so the money-hogging rat race **is** the national policy by default and with dire consequences. These dire consequences are things like corruption, greed, gross income inequality, the undermining and manipulation of democracy by the rich,

We have been conditioned to look upon the rich powerful countries as models. Why should these rich powerful countries be the model for the world with their history of slavery, colonialism, imperialism, hundreds of thousands of innocent people killed by their wars, their slaughter and dispossession of indigenous people all over the world. In God's name, why?

Forget them. Let us be different. Don't look elsewhere. In the words of Afro-American author Alice Walker," *we are the ones we have been waiting for*". With Goodwillism as our national policy, it will improve every aspect of Jamaica life. So, by enlisting Jamaicans in the Goodwill Revolution, we can make Jamaica the most desirable country in the world. Jamaica must lead the way and serve as a model for the rest of the developing world to follow.

www.ingramcontent.com/pod-product-compliance
Lightning Source LLC
Chambersburg PA
CBHW031304060726
47590CB00003B/1057